Executives:
Making Them Click

JOSEPH DEAN EDWARDS

Member of the New York Bar
Consultant to Management

Illustrations by Irwin Feher

WILDSIDE PRESS

Third Printing

To the memory of my grandmother
— My first coach

Executives: Making Them Click

Preface

This book had its inception in hundreds of consultations with sincere, brilliant, but perplexed executives who sometimes feel insecure, somewhat bitter, and genuinely concerned—because they or the management people they supervise are not operating at their highest level of effectiveness.

It received its impetus in a week when my schedule included:

(a)   A conference with the vice-president of an eminently successful business—one of three such meetings regularly scheduled each month to consider current and anticipated business problems. This consultation ran far over the usual period, and was devoted almost entirely to his sudden decision that what the company needed most was new blood in its executive levels. Would I give priority attention to an immediate search in the industry for men with proven executive ability to step into executive posts soon to be available or which would be newly created?

(b)   A consultation—at his request—with one of the men who was currently reporting to this vice-president. The man was completely frustrated, completely unhappy in his job. He had, in his own words, been stagnating for two years because the vice-president insisted on handling all the responsibility in his department, hog-tied his assistants with routine assignments offering no scope, no opportunity for growth. The man was ambitious, felt trapped.

Should he now sacrifice the years he had invested in his company, look around for a position with another company? And how could he insure that the same situation would not recur in his new post?

(c)   A luncheon meeting with a top executive of another company—and a good friend—whose head was indeed bending low. Why? He had just fired a member of his management staff—after two years of continual and futile effort to fit him into the organization. "You know," he told me, "that little experiment has cost the company at least $100,000 on the most conservative possible figuring. What caused my judgment to go so far off in this case?"

(d)   A meeting with the three top executives of a new client company. The company had quadrupled its sales in a two-year period just ending, with prospects of further growth in the immediate future. Its rapid expansion urgently required up-dating of its rudimentary organizational setup. "We want the works," declared the proud president, "organizational charts, replacement schedules, a management development program, evaluation forms —everything all the other companies have in this area."

(e)   Participation as a speaker and panel member in an all-day conference on executive problems. The question-and-answer period which followed each speech displayed over and over the same request, couched of course in different terms each time: What's the formula for converting men into good executives?

There is nothing more exciting than watching a good executive in action—unless it's watching him in action, knowing that you helped to produce him.

It's my sincere hope that this book will help to spread that excitement.

JOSEPH DEAN EDWARDS

New York, N. Y.
March 12, 1956

Contents

Executives: Making Them Click

Chapter 1

The Executive Development Myth

Since the end of World War II, there has been growing in the business world a myth more marvelous than any ever conceived by Messrs. Barnum and Bailey. This myth has already cost incalculable sums in wasted time and energy of the best brains in business. It has produced reams of literature; a sea of speeches; more seminars, forums, advanced-study-courses and what-have-you's than Jules Verne ever imagined. What's the myth? It is called "Executive Development Programs." It commands priority attention from top management all the way down the line. It has its own vocabulary, its own experts. And with each passing day, it becomes more king-size, more formidable, more costly . . . and what's much worse, more ineffective.

How did it all happen? Very simply. The end of the war brought a tremendous burst of business activity—all the business dammed up "for the duration" plus all the expansion needed to build the postwar dream. But, just at the moment when they were most needed to direct this activity, the overworked and overage executives who had been holding the fort suddenly began falling apart.

1

It would be difficult to find a single company which did not lose at least one key man to death or retirement during that period. "So, all right, let's promote the man under him and get going." Surprise! What man? For one reason or another (and they were generally very good reasons), he turned out to be the little man who wasn't there. Then began a period of raiding—when not a few executives changed their business address almost as frequently as their shirts. It was painful; it was expensive; it was sometimes unethical. But it was done. Eventually the key posts were more or less "covered" and business went roaring ahead to set its still astonishing records.

Then came a lull. Decisions had been made, policy set. The men who a few months before couldn't begin to clear their desks now found themselves with periods of leisure. These top-level executives then began to do what top-level executives do with leisure: they began to think. They thought about business; about their jobs; about their associates. And in a surprising number of companies, these executives used their new leisure to regret bitterly some of the hasty action which had been taken to fill executive openings in their companies. Mistakes had been made. These were now very painful to live with—very, very painful to get rid of. Tangibly and intangibly, the company had already suffered losses because of these mistakes—losses which would continue, perhaps even multiply, if the mistakes could not be neutralized quickly. It would be very nice indeed if such mistakes could be avoided in the future.

But how? What was the "magic formula"? These clever men knew there was no magic formula for solving their *other* business problems—no magic formula for increasing sales, developing new products, boosting production, cutting costs, maintaining quality standards, developing new markets, improving their company's competitive position. In these areas, each company's problems were individual, and required individual investigation and handling. What had worked for a competitor might be all wrong for us. However, on this executive problem, that's a different story. There we've all got the same problems—they're all human beings, aren't they?— and we can use the same solutions. All we have to do is find a

company which has the best formula—and copy it in our company.
A cinch!

The topic was brought up at executive lunch tables. It found
its way into management publications. Soon everybody was working on a program. Management charts were devised, borrowed,
improved on. Forms were devised for Executive Selection, Executive
Appraisal, and Executive Evaluation. After many conferences,
memoranda and directives, an executive development program was
installed with due ceremony—and another problem was licked.

Or was it? A lot of time and money has been going into these
programs. They have been in operation for several years. Are they
producing efficient, capable administrators, able to handle responsible jobs, able to train their assistants, able to move on to more
responsible positions as they open up? Rarely. In the vast majority
of companies, the management development program is a farce . . .
or worse, it is a fraud! It pretends to offer a formula for advancement when in fact it is only accidentally involved in the actual
process of advancement in the company. In company after company, the thoughtful executive who watches the program in
operation characterizes it quite simply: "It's window dressing."

Up and down and across the country, there are men in executive
positions who are learning how to work with people, how to
organize departments, how to get work done better, quicker,

cheaper. They are learning, in short, how to be better executives—but they are learning this despite the existence of an "executive development program" in their companies. Other men are standing still, or more accurately, are regressing in their jobs—despite their enthusiastic and conscientious adherence to a development program. A man in the second group may be currently far more valuable to his company than a man in the first group—he may even have a far greater potential—but he will reach his ceiling at a level below his real potential unless he is rescued.

The myth of today's executive development program is simply the belief that it is a magic formula, which, properly used, will produce brilliant, effective executives in the precise quantity and at the precise time when they are needed. Good executives can't be mass-produced and they shouldn't!

No *program* can do magic. People—*only people*—can do magic. And that is the point. There is no push-button system. You're interested not in executive *development*—not in a program: you're interested in developing *executives*—in people—your people, those who have already worked well and hard for you. And you do it one person at a time. And you do it differently for each person. With one man you will work carefully, unobtrusively. With another, you will work openly and with entire frankness. One man you will beat over the head with his mistakes—he doesn't bruise easily—that's how he learns. To another man, you will *never* use the word "mistake"—he's too brittle, too insecure—instead you look for an opportunity to suggest an experiment: "This time, let's see how this procedure would work."

That's your executive development program: your executives and would-be executives, plus the methods you must use to help each one to do a better job. No other company can have a pattern of progress just like yours—because no one else has your company and your executives to work with. Simple—but watch the results when you take out the myth and put in the magic in developing executives.

How is it done? The only way it can be done: top management must preach *and practice* the policy of helping its management people to grow. Top management itself must make continuing, conscious and directed efforts, day-in and day-out, to exploit fully every developmental opportunity which arises in the course of the business routine. It must look at every business luncheon, every business conference, every business contact at whatever level with this thought: "Could John or Jim or Bill learn something if he came along?" More than this, top management must exert constant and unrelenting pressure on middle management to adopt and practice the same policy—and so on down the management scale. This is the only tried and true way to produce capable executives: give each bright candidate ever more challenging opportunities to sharpen his skills and to learn to work effectively as a member of an executive team.

Not a pleasant chore? Will this interfere too much with your established routine? If so, and you're fully satisfied with what you now have and what's ahead in your present scheme of things— then—there is little point to reading this book.

Chapter II

Your Executive Floor —

Is It Clicking?

The vice-president had put in a rough morning and was still tied up in conference when his son arrived for a scheduled birthday luncheon. Told his dad would be through in about a half-hour, he decided to prowl around a bit. When he got back upstairs, his dad was just about ready to leave. Over lunch, the executive asked about his son's tour of inspection. He got an enthusiastic account of several of the office machines his son had inspected thoroughly. Then there was a pause, and this further comment: "Dad, you know, things are so much more alive in the other departments, downstairs. They feel as though they're really clicking!"

This executive likes to use this little story because it always gets a good reception. Executives seem to recognize it. They are less in accord on how to deal with it. The executive floor in more than one company seems to be in a state of suspended animation. Individual executives may be working at high speed, but there is no feeling on the floor of team effort—of people working together to get things done. A company cannot secure the maximum contribution of which its management people are capable until it welds them into a smoothly operating management team. Individual executives may be brilliant, but they cannot function at top efficiency when they are working "on their own." Accomplishment of company plans and goals requires group effort and group coöperation.

A company whose management is not working as a team will find it worth-while to look into situations which may be acting as blocks to the development of team spirit. Most of them exist to some degree in every company.

Provincialism at Top Levels?

Every business must continually evaluate its position in terms of two questions: How do we stand competitively? Where ought we stand? In that context, management deficiencies which involve the performance of the executive team as a whole emerge in these characteristic forms:

1.   Failure to hold or increase the company's share of the market.

2.   Failure to build up the product line or develop new lines.

3.   Failure to anticipate and meet effectively foreseeable problems or situations.

4.   Failure to keep abreast of technological progress in the industry or in related industries.

5.   Failure to see and move quickly to grasp opportunities for profits.

6.   Failure to understand and operate in line with economic, so-

cial and political developments impinging on the business or its operations.

The root of these and similar problems is the same: *lack of vision*. Men in management posts are not thinking outside the confines of their day-to-day operations. They are not leading the company in the direction of growth and profitable operation under *future* conditions. Their decisions and actions are being taken solely in the light of current operating circumstances. Some of the people in the top spots may not realize what is happening because their outlook is genuinely limited. Or, they may realize the situation but lack the opportunity or the courage, perhaps, to try to remedy matters. Whatever the reason, the business continues to operate *in the same old way* without regard to the dynamic, changing business environment.

A mere listing of the various factors which management must take into account in making policy decisions gives some picture of this staggering problem: technological influences, occupational changes, changes in levels of income and prices, the rise of "lifo" method of inventory accounting, the rise of the guaranteed wage, self-service arrangements in chain stores and supermarkets, rise of suburbia, movement of industry into outlying areas, new developments in setting work standards by time studies, growth of automation and "automatic brain" machinery, geographical shifts in population, effect of taxation on profits and income, changes in product packaging, rise of vending machines, increasing tendency of administrative agencies to "legislate," effects of regulatory policies of government on many business practices, changing policies and influence of labor unions, growing recognition of the importance of human relations skills in management, new methods of compensating executives by deferred compensation or stock option plans, and a million more. Small wonder if some decisions are made without reference to *every* pertinent factor.

Failure to think in broad terms is present to some degree in every member of your management team. Many men have risen to top jobs through their specialties and have never altogether broken the habit of thinking within the limits of those specialties.

Some of them, indeed, tell you proudly they still "keep up" with developments in their special fields. Some men have an unbalanced background of knowledge or experience—an executive who has no sales experience, for example—which affects their management thinking. Some executives in key positions are so cautious and opposed to risk-taking that they render an entire organization inflexible, unable to move quickly to take advantage of an opportunity for profits and growth.

In companies where the management group is small, executives may have to assume responsibilities in several divergent fields. In such cases, an executive may be continually forced to shift his attention from sales to personnel, to production, to merchandizing, to finance, to public relations, and so on through the gamut. The capacity for making such quick mental shifts day-in, day-out is far from common—as is the blend of knowledge and experience necessary for effective operation under such circumstances.

If management thinking and planning seem pedestrian in your company, you might analyze the underlying causes along these lines:

1.   Is there one man in a top position whose lack of vision or daring is paralyzing the thinking of the rest of the management group?

2.   If so, can he be vitalized, given a broader view of his responsibilities to the company? Or, alternatively, can he be placed in a position where he can act as a valuable brake, but not a block, to the broad-gauge thinking and planning of the others?

3.   If there is not a single, conspicuous roadblock at present, does the existing cautious, limited viewpoint stem from an overpowering executive in the recent past whose influence still insensibly controls the group?

4.   Are there interpersonal rivalries which are absorbing the attention of the members of the management group to the detriment of the business?

5.   Are there too many men in the group who rose to top jobs by not making any mistakes, rather than by positive action?

6.   Is executive quality second-rate because the road to promotion is so long that top-flight men don't sit it out?

7. Are the men overabsorbed in the details and trivia of running their departments or operations?

8. Did too many men rise to top positions on the basis of seniority alone?

A company in which even one important management post is held by a man of limited outlook may find that the work of management is done in the midst of constant battle. The rest of the team may get projects through but only after bucking the roadblock. Usually this means that a few valuable plans get voted down—in effect sacrificed, so that other more important plans can be put through. Almost invariably, this situation also develops or encourages politics among the executive team: coalitions forming for or against projects on the basis of personal advancement rather than on the basis of objective merit. When this goes on long enough, even removal of the roadblock will not mean a smoothly operating team since the divisions have existed too long.

Too Many Bosses—or None?

In some companies the executive floor consists of a collection of bosses who wear themselves out trying to boss each other. The basic difficulty is that the executive jobs are like Topsy—they just grew. As new responsibilities came along, they were assigned to people more or less arbitrarily: "He's been doing a good job; let's give him a crack at this." "It seems to fall within his department." "He has time to take care of it." No one has really looked at the executive job as a whole, or attempted to assign executive responsibilities within some logical framework. Result?

1.   There is duplication or overlapping of functions. Several executives may have responsibilities, vaguely outlined, in the same general area. Some matters are handled by three people, each working independently and in ignorance of the efforts of the others; some matters are not handled at all.

2.   Levels of authority are not clearly defined. The same man may be handling responsibilities at several levels of the organization structure, uncertain himself just where he stands in the organization. In fact, the level of his job may vary depending on who is handling the job at a particular time.

3.   Some important responsibilities may not be specifically assigned. In a fluid situation, each member of management tends to concentrate his energies in those areas which he can handle best. If his choice conflicts with that of another management man, some rough working arrangement usually results, with inevitably some fuzzy areas in between which neither man handles. If conditions are right, this arrangement may result in costly and wasteful jockeying for position. Again, some responsibilities are over-handled, others neglected.

4.   Some men handle too many responsibilities. Sometimes the problem is purely overwork; sometimes it grows out of the fact that the man is handling a hodgepodge of activities, only vaguely connected. If related activities were coördinated and placed under a single man, perhaps two or three others would be relieved of partial responsibilities which required all of them to keep informed of the same matters.

5.   Some management men do not have the authority they need to handle their responsibilities effectively. The trouble may be that a superior does not want to relinquish his control. Or the executive himself may be using the situation as a convenient excuse for his lack of effectiveness in his job.

6.   Some executives have more men reporting to them than

they can supervise effectively. Most companies have found that a top executive should not have more than five to seven men reporting to him—fewer if the management people are carrying heavy loads. Supervisors of people doing routine work, on the other hand, can effectively manage as many as twenty men.

7. Some executives report to more than one superior. Even if he handles two entirely separate jobs, it is usually better to have him report to only one superior. He receives better supervision and better training when responsible to one man at a time.

These blocks to effective management teamwork require corrections in the organization structure. If too many of the management people are overworked, more executive positions may have to be created to take up the overflow. Perhaps some executive jobs should be broken up. Perhaps another level of executive jobs should be created—"assistant-to" jobs—which would serve both to take some of the routine work off the executive's hands and to train a backstop for his position.

Many companies start by holding a conference with all management people at which organizational distortions are explored, tentative solutions are worked out. This method has two drawbacks: (1) the amount of management time required for such a conference with resultant interference with operations; (2) personality difficulties may complicate the discussions, stall solutions. Another method which avoids these difficulties is to have someone not directly involved in a possible reorganization make a preliminary study of the immediate problem areas, list possible solutions. Generally, the person making this study is a management consultant. His report is circulated among all management people and a first meeting is held at which their reactions are aired. A second meeting is then scheduled at which decisions are reached. The drawback in the second method is simply its cost. Whatever method is used, the point is to secure substantial agreement by the management group on both the desirability of an organizational change, and the change itself.

Executive Team—or Executive Stars?

Some companies, like the early movie studios, operate on the star system. They depend on the talents of one, perhaps two, outstanding executives, rather than on the combined knowledge and experience of their executive team. These executives are usually brilliant men, well-respected and tremendously productive. In drive and effectiveness, they far outshine their associates. It is entirely natural for the company to want them to handle the "sticky" management problems. Difficulties arise when more and more of the management problems are labeled "sticky" and are routed to their desks. Sometimes, also, it isn't the company but the executive himself who creates the situation. In either case, the real work of management is being handled by a "star," not by a team. And there are some very obvious, serious disadvantages:

1. Regardless of how efficient the man may be, it isn't long before he is trying to handle an impossible workload. The perpetual grind prevents the executive from finding a fresh, creative approach to a problem—yet that's the very reason the problem is on his desk. Also, the overloading must inevitably result in fatigue, narrowing of the man's perspective, even affect his health.

2. With all important matters automatically shunted to a single executive, the rest of the team in effect become his assistants, rather than his associates. They will be handling only those routine or nonimportant matters which the "star" cares to delegate. Their opportunities for growth are necessarily limited since they are forever clearing things with him rather than exercising their own judgment and making their own mistakes. Those with best potential leave for more fruitful pasture.

3. The man's blind spots in qualifications or experience assume tremendous importance. They will result time and again in decisions based on inadequate or erroneous information, or on improper evaluation of information. The effects of these blind spots cannot be neutralized or minimized as happens in other companies because the executive is in effect running a one-man show.

The weakness of a management team on which there is such a star costs the company more in hopelessly wasted managerial talent than the star's most brilliant efforts are worth. What to do? How preserve for the company the star's undeniably valuable contribution without permitting him to harm the management team? There are at least two solutions:

1.   Give the man a top-flight managerial post which permits him to do important work, but in addition to, rather than instead of, the work of the management team.

2.   Make him a consultant—with perhaps only one client, your company. Let him then devote his efforts to the problems at which he does so well, but without upsetting the executive organization in which he is a misfit.

Always Open Season . . .

Many companies encourage a spirit of competition on their executive floor: "Keeps the men on their toes." Carried too far, though, the men never get off their toes to do any running. They spend at least as much time guarding themselves from attack as they do in actual management work. And the criterion quickly becomes not "which action might get the best results"—but "which action will keep me from being criticized." Members of management are so busy jockeying for position they have little time left over to run the company.

Even if top executives do not actually have this philosophy, their executive staff may still spend much of their time and energy on the defensive. The climate or atmosphere on the executive floor may be the cause. Basically, there may be no real contact between the various levels of management people other than in the setting of standards. Lower-level people work under the pressure of having to meet those standards, but without an assurance that they will be *helped* to meet the standards when the help from above is legitimately needed. Frequently, neither the lower-level nor the upper-level executives know in what situations help should be forthcoming from above. Hence the atmosphere on the executive floor is tense, partly because of unnecessary uncertainty, partly because of unnecessary fear of failure. Men don't know when they are doing a good job. When their responsibilities are changed in any way, they are not really certain if this is a mark of achievement and promotion, or of criticism and demotion. And they are even afraid to ask—because the lack of knowledge thus betrayed *may* be a black mark against their record! What *may* be is made an artificial obstacle course.

An atmosphere of competitiveness may be created also from within the executive staff. One of the men may be overanxious to establish the merit of his work, whether for reasons of psychic insecurity or ambition to progress quickly. The method he often chooses is to compare his excellent work with that of another man's, which of course doesn't stack up as well in the particular instances he selects. If the man to whom such an executive reports does not immediately and emphatically discourage such comparisons, he will find the method repeated as often as the occasion arises. The other men, of course, will eventually realize what is happening, and probably will follow suit in pure self-defense.

Some executives excuse their acquiescence in such situations with the statement that it keeps them informed, as no other method could, of the actual shortcomings of their executive staff in action. They add that, of course, they form their own judgments after they have learned the facts of the situation. It is doubtful, however, if the knowledge gained is worth the price it costs in division and dissension among the executive team. These executives could secure the same information—while at the same time creating opportunities for building up their people—by promoting an atmosphere of confidence in their desire to be constructive where situations may be a little too much for their people to handle. They would still see the shortcomings of their man in action—but, in addition, they might get some insight into the *causes* of the man's shortcomings.

There are some executives who, while discouraging talebearing on ethical grounds, genuinely do not understand that such a situation reveals deficiencies in their *own* performance. They give their people a free hand in performing their responsibilities, and feel that it is up to each man to *prove* himself. If he does, of course, there will be no tales to bear back to them. So, as they analyze the situation, talebearing means that some man is not doing his job properly, and another man is sharp enough to realize it. The result is that while ostensibly they rebuke the man who carries the tale, actually they feel it is to the man's credit that he recognizes situations which need improvement. More often than not, the interview may end with some gesture which is in effect a reward to the man for his good work.

How does talebearing reveal the executive's own deficiencies? In several ways: *First,* by adopting the attitude that his men must *prove* themselves, the executive is in effect falling down on one of the most important aspects of his job. He is acting as Judge. He should be acting as Coach. If the man reporting to an executive has nothing to learn from him, that man should have the executive's job. Otherwise, his talents are being wasted. *Second,* if the executive has to learn about his people's shortcomings through tales, it indicates that he hasn't done a good job of appraising his people. If he had, he would already be aware of their shortcomings and would know how they should be expected to act in given situations. *Third,* if the executive has to learn about mishandled situations through tales, it indicates not only a lack of communication—but a lack of control. A good manager is "on top of things" in his department. If he doesn't know what's going on, he's not doing his own job properly. *Fourth,* since talebearers carry bad news, the executive certainly won't hear from them about other people's triumphs. His communications downwards will thus tend to be confined to negative or critical comments—the classic complaint: "He never has a compliment to spare when we do good work, but we sure hear about it in spades when something goes wrong."

White-Haired Boys

It is the rare firm which is not, in at least one instance, attempting to make an executive out of a "sow's ear." The reasons are immaterial. Sometimes men have gone up the executive ladder by the sheer chance of being in the right spot when a job became vacant. Sometimes seniority is the reason: the man's superior simply funked the unpleasant job of putting a halt to the man's progress, salving his conscience with the assurance that the superior at the next level would do so. Occasionally, men rise through inheritance, marriage, or judicious and skillful "apple-polishing" despite inferior management skills. Whatever the reason, the result is the same: a man is in a management post which he is incapable of handling properly. His presence is a drag on the performance of the entire management team: other men will have to do his work in addition to their own. At best, there is always the vague feeling that his area of responsibility is not up to par.

Where such a man is in the upper levels of management, the only palatable solution may be to kick him still further upstairs— into a position which in effect has him making speeches instead of running the company. Or, he may be transferred laterally into a position where his deficiencies are largely neutralized because of the work he is handling.

Where such a man is in middle management, the problem is more difficult to solve. If his performance in his current post is by and large satisfactory, though not outstanding, the company may decide to leave him there—permanently. Should he be told that he has reached his ceiling? That depends on the man. Some can face up to the situation, continue to do good work. Others would fall apart if told bluntly they have no place to go in the company; even if eventually they begin to suspect this, they will continue to function satisfactorily as long as they can find reasons for not moving ahead.

If an executive's present performance is too inadequate to be allowed to continue, the company really has a painful job. He must be replaced. But the axe job has to be done without destroying the man, and without leaving behind a shocked and demoralized executive staff. One solution is to "blink" the whole problem by wangling for the executive a responsible post in another company which he could handle successfully—and thus give him a chance to bow out gracefully. Failing that, the man can be offered a less responsible job in another location, perhaps another city. Such demotions are rarely successful, however, because of the delicate problems of human relations involved.

Executive failures are tragic and costly, and their effects linger on long after the incident has been closed. Properly analyzed, however, they may provide valuable guides to the company in future selection and training of executives. Why did the man fail? Could his failure have been foreseen from an accurate appraisal of his personality and qualifications? Had he been given sufficient experience in backstopping the previous occupant of the post? What was his record in his previous jobs? Are conditions such that the same sort of mistake could happen again?

We've Always Done It This Way . . .

One of the most serious shortcomings of management people is their increasing tendency, as they rise in executive circles, to "stand pat." Why take chances? Why experiment with a new method which *may* work better but which just may not? The higher the man stands in management, the more embarrassing is each mistake. Since chances of being criticized for *not* doing something are far less than for acting, how much smarter to take it easy! If things are handled in the time-honored tradition, and go wrong . . . well, that's the breaks; you can't win them all. If things are handled in some new way, and go wrong . . . well, maybe they wouldn't have if the time-tested procedures had been followed; was there really any good reason to depart from them?

Multiply this attitude by the number of matters with which each such executive deals each day—it then becomes easier to see the extent of nondynamic "thinking" within the management team.

Is it important? After all, how many matters coming across the executive's desk lend themselves to creative thinking? Few, probably. But could even one of these spark a fresh viewpoint of the company, its services or its customers—*if* the executive's attitude were receptive? How often have we heard the story of the brilliant idea:

"It was one of my busiest days, everyone I saw had a problem, everything was going wrong, I was getting more impatient and dissatisfied by the minute. In the middle of all the mess, I suddenly found myself wondering how it would work if we did thus and so—instead of so and so. The thought had no connection whatever with my work at the moment, but it interested me and I began toying with the idea . . ."

No connection? or by-product? If his mind had not been playing in and around the people and the problems with which he was struggling, would it have produced the spark? If he had been merely plodding doggedly through the routine, applying standard practices and procedures, would he have recognized the spark, developed it into a workable idea?

Executives who continually work in the old ways eventually come to prefer the old ways. It's so easy. Without in the least intending to, they begin to resist changes, resist even examining them for possible merit. They tend to cling to pet ideas or time-tested theories. When changes do occur, their adjustment is dangerously slow and frequently accompanied by emotional disturbance. Sometimes, even, they unconsciously obstruct the installation or operation of new methods of which they do not approve.

If such men are in the upper levels of management, it isn't hard to understand why some companies are always in the rear guard, rather than the vanguard, of their industries. Can this represent the difference between merged into as against merged with?

Goals—Too Many? or None?

It would be hard to find an executive who hasn't occasionally asked himself, in some anguish, just what he's supposed to be doing, for pete's sake. Such introspective periods frequently follow executive meetings—at which progress to date of the various departments and projects is assessed, new plans and projects are formulated. At each such meeting, the executive is apt to get a different version of what his "most important job" for the next period is supposed to be. And since, not infrequently, the new goal is not consistent with the goals previously set for him, but is to be pursued in conjunction with the previous ones, the executive is understandably perturbed.

Sometimes, by application of clear, cold logic, he can analyze the situation sufficiently to discover that actually the same goal is being set—only the language or the approach is different. However, more often than not, the executive can't do such an analysis—because he doesn't have enough information with which to work. He then has a choice: (a) try to get more information, if he can; or (b) don't worry about understanding why, just get hopping on the new line.

Either course is fraught with perils, both to the executive and to the company. If he tries to get more information, he may find himself labeled as uncoöperative, slow on the uptake, presumptuous in assuming his superior's decisions need explanation or examination. If he skips the background and merely tries to execute the new policy, he may find later on that he misunderstood the policy, or interpreted it incorrectly since he did not have proper background information which he should have tried to get. Of course, the company suffers either from the waste of his efforts, or from the mistakes of his misdirected efforts.

Not much teamwork in this situation. If the efforts of the executives were to be charted, they would represent a series of lines leading nowhere, rather than a short direct line to a goal. Unfortunately, there are many companies who would have to admit that the first chart is more representative of their own operations than the second.

How can executives work as a team unless the members of the team know precisely what their contributions should be? What are executive meetings for except to communicate to each member of the team that precise knowledge? What's wrong with the climate of a company if an executive who doesn't understand his role either can't or doesn't try to find out? Is the problem of too many goals in reality a problem of no goals? Are executive personalities acting or reacting upon each other destructively rather than constructively?

Well, perhaps the executive floor is missing a few "clicks" here and there. Maybe the tempo needs some jacking up. How does a company go about it? What do you have to do to make the executive floor work as a top-flight team? What does any coach do—first, get good men on the team; second, teach them to work together as a team.

Getting good men on the team comes first. Most of these we'll find in the ranks and we'll bring them up; each according to his tempo; his inner strength; his ability to coach and be coached.

Some of the members of the team will be new to the company, but they won't be new for very long—not if they're selected and introduced into the company with team play as the keynote.

Let's look at some of the men who usually won't make the team and why. In our next chapter let's see, too, what we *can* do for them and for the company, by a review of several case histories. Do you recognize them?

Chapter III

Your Executives—
Are They Clicking?

The executive who isn't clicking is not in every case clearly or easily recognizable. It's not a simple matter of putting the finger on the man who cost the company $40,000 because of a wrong decision last week—he may recoup that amount twice over next week by a brilliantly correct decision. Every executive makes many decisions and some of them will necessarily be "wrong" in light of subsequent events. The man can't be labeled as not clicking merely on the basis of his "right" and "wrong" score.

Sometimes, the executive who isn't clicking looks remarkably like Richard Graves, your hardest-working, most productive, most conscientious guy . . . that is, on the surface. There's nothing wrong with either the quality or the quantity of Richard's results . . . that is, on the surface. The only tip-off to the fact that there is something wrong with the way Richard is clicking is his increased tenseness—a danger signal which immediately alerts his wise superior to the need for closer attention to what's going on with Richard.

23

At times, the executive who isn't clicking looks more like Peter Adams, your model department head, whose people turn in fabulously perfect work, whose own performance is superlatively outstanding . . . that is, on the surface. The only tip-off to Peter's superior is the puzzling sterility of Peter's department—no bright "comers" ever seem to come from there—a sure sign that there's something very wrong with the way Peter is clicking.

As you look at Richard and Peter and the other executives profiled in this chapter, consider not only the *clues* which should alert management to inadequate executive performance, but the *methods* by which management must uncover these hidden clues.

WEEKEND !

He's Always So Busy

Richard Graves is fairly tall, of medium build, wears well-made clothes of conservative type. He has shrewd eyes, a sharp, quick mind, great charm and ease of manner, an infectious laugh which comes easily on social occasions. He is a creative thinker, always a step or two ahead of the rest of the management group. He occupies a top post in his company, but his influence is even greater because of his personal friendship with the "boss." He works late two or three evenings a week, always carries a bulging briefcase. He gets along on three or four hours of sleep, his last vacation was three years ago, cut short after one week because he was badly needed to help launch a new project. He is an unofficial coördinator of the activities of several departments, spends most of his day in conferences. The men who work for Richard are hand-picked, bright, ambitious. They find him hard to please but unstinting in praise of a good job. His door is always open to them for advice and assistance—although most of the time he's either not there or is constantly interrupted by a stream of telephone and personal callers. His people, in desperation, have resorted to an official "late night"—when they all stay, have dinner with Richard and thrash out with him the problems they are having in their work. Richard runs all the time, very often skips lunch, gets tense and wound up, expects people to understand his short temper at such times. And always there are huge stacks of work waiting to get done, and handled mostly at night or on week ends (he's started coming to the office on Saturdays in the past year, to try to make a dent on the piles). His boss worries about Richard. He needs him desperately; doesn't like the tension-and-temper periods which are coming more often lately; doesn't like the way Richard drives his people when he's busy; especially doesn't like the way he drives himself. Richard has been withdrawing more and more from activities in his home community (can't spare the time); seems to grasp eagerly at more and more responsibility despite an already overwhelming schedule; continues to do tremendously fine work while becoming more and more tense and brittle; more conscious of his car stalling; more impatient with the "little things."

Every organization has an executive who "lives" his job. Early and late, he's plugging away at his desk; lugs that bulging briefcase back and forth; breaks reluctantly for meals and then buries himself again in his work. Before you jump to the conclusion that he is overloaded and conscientious, probe a little. Is it possible that in his case (like in Richard's case), the overwork is necessary to fill a psychic need? In Richard's case, the problem is known both to Richard and his boss:

Difficulties at home. Richard meets an unhappy domestic situation by burying himself in his job. It's not a healthy situation but his boss hesitates to meddle. He and Richard are personal friends, have talked a bit about the situation. To Richard, a divorce is no solution because he has children of whom he is very fond and to whom he feels he owes an unbroken home. His wife finds her outlets in community activities—she's a very bright, very active person, contributes much help to her husband and to his firm by these social activities. But the home is not happy, and Richard comes back to work after week ends so markedly tense the entire staff has learned to avoid him on Monday morning, if possible; his work continues at a high level, but his health undoubtedly is beginning to suffer. In addition, Richard's boss wonders about the effect on Richard's staff.

To attempt to force Richard to give up his chosen outlet might be to risk losing his services entirely. To let him go on might have the same effect. Richard's boss has decided, on the basis of his personal friendship, to speak bluntly, advise Richard to see a psychiatrist for possible help. He's counting on the fact that he has worked along with the situation for three years, has seen it become steadily more wearing upon Richard, can point to specific instances of "illness" which were directly caused by home disturbances: he's relying on these factors to offset Richard's possible resentment and get his coöperation.

It may not be that easy in other cases. Overwork may be a response to other psychic needs besides home problems, such as:

Insecurity. The man may be fully competent, satisfactory in every way. But he may *feel* that he isn't doing as well as he should because of unrealistic standards or goals he has set for himself. Such men are usually unable to distinguish between these fanciful standards of their own, and the more reasonable objective standards by which their performance is actually judged. They are bitter and resentful and upset nervously because they feel they have failed— and all of this of course is unacknowledged even to themselves. The constant feverish overwork is an unconscious attempt to compensate for the fancied inadequacy.

Such men wouldn't necessarily be a problem for anyone but themselves—except that the feelings of inadequacy and insecurity frequently lead to physical ailments. The troubled emotions must find an outlet eventually, and in many men the outlet will be in physical illness which is not necessarily connected with the emotional turmoil—abdominal ailments, heart disease or similar illnesses. When this happens, it will usually take much professional assistance to rehabilitate the man and place him back in productive use of his faculties and energies.

Need for approval.　Some men can't function properly without a pat on the back from the boss after a job well done. If they don't get it, they assume it's because the job is not done well. They respond by working longer and harder, driving themselves and their staff into impossible workloads, thus creating unsatisfactory work, and starting the whole cycle over again.

Recognition that such men need tangible evidence of approval by their superiors doesn't necessarily involve babying them. Frequently, the recognition itself will change the atmosphere. A superior who habitually employs gruff tones and abrupt orders will naturally tend to temper them if he recognizes their effect on such personalities—and this alone, without the direct approving statement, may be enough to remove the tension upon such men.

These instances are obviously only a sampling of the diverse human factors which may be impelling your overworked executive to carry his staggering load. If you suspect this explanation exists in a particular case, proceed cautiously. Careful probing may give you a clue to a situation you can handle—something in his work environment which you can change for his benefit. If his difficulty seems deep-seated, however, it is always wiser to let the professionals take over. How to get him to the professional? One company handled the problem very neatly: It asked all its key people to submit to a complete physical examination, adding as an afterthought that this included consultation with a psychiatrist. The two men whom the company wanted to refer never suspected the maneuver was staged for their benefit.

He Won't Let You Handle Things

Allan Reed holds an executive position as assistant to one of the top men in his company. The job is rated as a "plum" and Allan had to weather stiff competition to get the appointment. His boss is a brilliant, talented executive who has his finger in every pie. As his assistant, Allan has learned a great deal about how a company is run, what the problems are with which executives at top levels must contend, how facts and figures are collected and projected for future planning. He sits in on top-level conferences, sees decisions hammered out, observes how activities at different levels are coördinated for the most efficient and profitable operation of the business.

However, Allan is really a bystander. He has only nominal responsibilities, no real authority to do anything more than initial routine handling of matters. Every real decision must be referred back to his boss who actually takes action. Allan's real job is to investigate matters under instructions from his boss, write reports or recommendations for his boss to use in making the decision. Frequently, his boss makes the decision without any attempt to indicate to Allan why he chose one course of action in preference to another. Allan works under the chafing frustration of handling bits and pieces of problems, but with no real matters of his own to handle from start to finish, making his own decisions and seeing them carried out.

Allan's boss may be one of the men who find it impossible to give over even a small part of the reins of authority to someone else. This is true even though he appears to delegate responsibilities to Allan. Actually, he retains all real authority, merely gives Allan a research job. He uses Allan the way he would an office boy.

The excuse of many nondelegating executives that their subordinates simply won't work satisfactorily without adequate supervision doesn't hold water in most cases. Errors will be made, of course. But the executive can just as effectively control operations by periodic checks as by having every decision referred to him directly. The only real relief from mounting job pressure is delegation—transferring some responsibilities, with their duties *and* authority—to subordinates.

Matters which arrive at the executive's desk for handling will usually fall into one of three categories: (a) those involving recurring or routine situations, (b) those involving emergencies, or (c) those involving long-range implications. To delegate effectively, the executive should handle questions which fall into group (a) just once—by setting a policy or establishing a precedent. Similar matters should then be handled by his subordinates within the terms of the policy or precedent. Matters which fall into group (b) are legitimately the executive's concern only where they involve a substantial change in established policy or have some long-range effect which may affect other decisions. Where they are purely operational problems, they should be brought to the executive only for his information, not for his handling. Questions which fall into group (c) are the essence of the executive's job. Actually, they are the only matters which should take his time and effort. And these are the only matters in which he should use his assistants to marshall facts or gather data without also making the decisions.

It isn't enough just to delegate, however. The executive must see to it that the assistant has enough knowledge or information to be able to handle the matters delegated. Also, he must back him up both on good work and on bad. When the assistant makes an error, obviously he must be held responsible. Authority to act carries with it responsibility for action taken. But having pointed out the mistake, the executive must then be sure that the assistant receives constructive criticism as well: he must show the man why it was a mistake and how to handle similar matters properly next time. If the executive merely limits his contribution to a scolding, the assistant will shortly avoid making decisions involving risk, look for *safe* ways to handle the work.

Insisting on delegation is a lot easier than making sure that delegation actually takes place. In one company, for example, a very able manager simply couldn't keep his hands off his department's operations. Although he nominally assigned responsibilities to his subordinates, he was always "on top of them," personally followed up every order, every decision. He never gave his people the opportunity to make mistakes and learn from them. They were expected to make decisions, but never knew when the boss might overrule or reverse their actions. The company tried this solution: it piled two big jobs on the executive to handle in addition to his regular work. Since he was the kind of person who took pride in doing the impossible, he undertook to do them both. They so absorbed his efforts that for six months he gave very little real attention to his own department—simply didn't have the time. He was forced to let his people run the operation. When he emerged, he found that his subordinates had done an excellent job, and for the first time was able to recognize their real competence. His company did not have to repeat the treatment a second time in his case.

Effective delegation is not a one-shot proposition. In day-to-day operations, new situations develop which make previous delegations unworkable or insufficient. Business growth may require appointment of more assistants, or may reveal inadequacy of present assistants to handle increased volume of work. At every level, executives must continually reëvaluate their workloads with the question: *"Can't Allan handle this instead of my doing it?"* Every "no" should be carefully examined with as much honesty as the executive can command. Why "no"? Because the job won't be handled as well? Not the first time or the second time, perhaps, but is the job that all-important when measured against the other uses to which the executive could put his time and energy? "No" because the executive likes to do the particular job involved? Again, does the job warrant use of his high-priced talents rather than those of lower-priced assistants? Such dollars-and-cents comparisons of the value of executive time compared with that of subordinates has proved very useful in even the most stubborn cases.

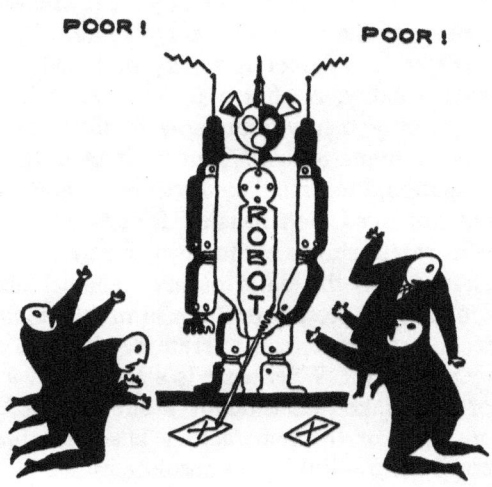

POOR! POOR!

He Isn't Coming Along As Well As Hoped

George Carr is slender, of medium height, with a pleasant, outgoing disposition. He seems sincere, trustworthy and warm; has a genuine interest in the people he works with. They find him always willing to listen, even if he can't help. He works steadily but quietly, gets things done. He is well-liked and well-respected by his associates, has the complete coöperation of his subordinates. For the past three years, he has been the understudy to the department head, Peter Adams. Recently, a question of promotion came up, and Peter discussed with the Home Office supervisor whether George was ready for consideration. Peter's verdict was that George was a disappointment. Although he did his work satisfactorily, he was coming along very slowly, still had a great deal to learn. He would need more seasoning before he would be ready for advancement.

The Home Office man was troubled. He had been counting on George to take over a good position in the Home Office. He looked over George's record again, wondered what was happening. He decided to stick around for a few days and observe George himself, while ostensibly installing a new program. He soon found himself observing not George, but George's boss, Peter Adams. Peter was the cause of George's lack of progress.

Peter is a forceful, stocky man, who gives the impression of great solidity. He has a squeaky voice but has learned to control it—it only betrays him now in times of stress. He is a man of violent inner tempers, but is outwardly well-controlled. He has exceptional technical competence, is much respected for his ability, but not liked, and has few friends. He is regarded as a cold fish who rarely shows enthusiasm, rarely has a good word to say for anyone. On the basis of his technical ability, he rose from the ranks to his present position in middle management. He has a per- fectionist nature, can tolerate no slightest error in the work which he supervises. Whether it is a letter with a single misspelled word, or a mistaken decision by a subordinate, the same furious storm breaks over the malefactor's head. He manages not by affection nor by fear—but by an absolute insistence on perfection, enforced by pettiness and sarcasm. He creates chaos in working schedules by constantly returning work to be redone because of minor im- perfections. Instead of using errors as an opportunity for training subordinates, he regards imperfect work as a personal reflection on the way he runs his department. He recognizes no excuses for a job poorly done, registers no appreciation for a job well done. He never makes a mistake himself (or at least never recognizes a mistake as his own), and expects others to be similarly perfect.

Because of his perfectionist nature, Peter has hidden resentments against his superiors whom he regards as less qualified than him- self. He feels bitterly that he is being held back from his rightful position in the company by men who are jealous of his achieve- ments, fearful that he will "show them up." His contacts with his subordinates, including George, are limited to weekly half-hour sessions at which he gives directions. He does not encourage George or anyone else to come into his office to ask for advice or help on job problems; preferring, instead, to check the finished product, point out mistakes, require it to be redone. Instead of coaching or counseling George, he keeps score on his perform- ance. He gives George no opportunity to learn anything except the routines, never discusses George's recommendations or reports, actively discourages George from trying to follow up. George, apparently, feels it is futile to buck City Hall, does the best he can under the circumstances.

The Home Office man has a tough problem. Peter's advancement is definitely limited by his own nature. Men like Peter who have no warmth can rarely be developed as effective administrators beyond a certain point. Peter's performance is genuinely outstanding in the field of his technical specialty. However, as a man whose job it is to get things done through the efforts of others, he is very poor. Lacking tolerance, he sacrifices his subordinates' enthusiasm and initiative to an overemphasized and mostly unnecessary goal of perfection. He actively discourages experimentation or a search for new methods. His men are so busy doing work over to eliminate minor and unimportant "mishandling," they haven't the time to do more than keep up with the routine. Although Peter is a good technical man, his people aren't because they don't get the experience of meeting situations on their own, making and learning from mistakes. All they do is to carbon-copy Peter to the best of their ability and without knowing why in most cases.

Because of his limitations, Peter can't advance further in management levels. But keeping him in his current position is equally bad for the organization. He is stifling and discouraging the growth of able subordinates who can't develop into more than passably adequate assistants as long as they must work under the weight of Peter's negative personality and inhuman standards. For the good of the organization, Peter should be "walled-off"—placed in a position where his good technical contribution can continue, but where he won't have responsibility for developing people, or more accurately, holding them back, as in the case of George.

He Never Gets Done

Jerry Andrews is a pleasant, agreeable man, rather short and heavy-set, with a nice smile. His eyes have a vague look, however, as if he were inwardly contemplating some problem. He finds it hard to relax even for a few minutes, frets at having to spend several hours a week at conferences and briefing sessions. And he complains all the time about being so busy he can't spare time for this or that. He comes in an hour early (to get some work done before the telephone starts in), leaves an hour or two late every night (trying to clean up), takes work home with him most evenings, every week end. He never seems to be without papers in his hands, carries a perpetual air of rush and hurry. Despite all this motion, however, his work is always behind schedule and his subordinates' work is equally behind. He and his whole department seem to work unceasingly and, occasionally, frantically, but with no real dent being made on the workload.

His company is concerned. In the perpetual grind to get through the work, Jerry sticks closely to the routines. He never seems to find time for a fresh, creative approach to a problem. Much quicker to do things the old way. But Jerry complains of monotony. Also, Jerry never has time any more to look around him at what's going on in the industry and in the world. His perspective has steadily narrowed so that in staff conferences other men have to point out certain implications of a course of action being discussed, although it is Jerry's job to see and advise on those implications. Jerry hasn't had the time or energy to keep up with things. For a while after such incidents, Jerry makes a superhuman effort to find time to attend trade meetings, read more than the papers which cross his desk. But shortly the inertia sets in again. Jerry's growth is definitely being limited while he himself is ridden by hurry and haste and chafing frustration.

The problem of overwork may be common to your whole management team. But the causes and cures will in most cases differ and must be looked at individually in each case. Why is Jerry, for example, so hampered by overwork? Is it because of:

Load of details?   One study showed that executives spend up to one-third of their time on detail work which should have been handled by subordinates . . . or shouldn't have been done at all. There are four principal causes:

(a) *Inadequate controls.* In one case, the executive spent a considerable amount of time running down inventory figures. This was obviously clerical work—but he had to do it simply because his company did not have a workable inventory control system.

(b) *Absence of standards.* His company had not established an inventory policy, setting inventory for each product. So, the executive on each occasion had to spend more time discussing the inventory figures with various of his associates, deciding which figures were too low, which too high.

(c) *Poor work organization.* Many executives spend countless hours signing things: checks, memos, interoffice notes, etc. Most, if not all, of this countersigning is unnecessary. The executive hasn't time to read the stuff—although presumably it comes to his desk for signature to insure his control. Much better to give responsibility to a subordinate who *will* read it, thus getting real rather than hoped-for control.

(d) *Bad work habits.* Since there's too much to do anyway, it seems to matter little how much time is spent on what. So the unimportant and the important get the same thorough attention or the same hurried lack of attention, despite their obviously different claims on the executive's time.

Poor working rhythm? All persons, executives included, have a definite working rhythm, but most men are only vaguely aware of that fact and don't, therefore, know how to take advantage of it. They know they feel a slump at certain times, but don't really pay attention either to the timing of the letdown, or to their reaction at that time.

As an experiment to discover how they really spent their working days, five executives in one company had their secretaries keep detailed diaries of their activities during one three-month period. The diaries on comparison revealed that each man experienced letdowns which followed a similar general pattern. One came around 10:30 or so in the morning; another—more severe—occurred right after lunch. At those times, each man took what he described as a "break." One man got on the telephone, visited around in his department. Another took up routine matters, not requiring concentration or fresh attention.

The weakness of such a working rhythm is not that executives feel fatigue or a letdown. It is that the means which the men chose to break their work rhythm tended to prolong the slump. Switching to routine chores, for example, meant frequently that the man went on plugging at them long after the need for a break was gone, and he should have gone back to his more pressing and exacting work. The man who visited around his department did further damage by disrupting the work of his subordinates.

The need for a break is real, but it should be recognized and used constructively. One man merely does this: a "don't disturb" sign goes up on his door and on his telephone; he takes a fifteen-minute rest on his office couch. Another listens to favorite recordings for a half-hour on his office record player. A third bats away on his golf ball in its mechanical device. In each case, the man is getting the essence of a break: turning from the work at hand to something wholly different. And, equally important, the break is kept under control and held to a specified period of time without disturbing the working rhythm of his subordinates.

Why Doesn't He Retire?

Fred Reynolds is a vigorous, active man in his sixties. He prides himself on his ability to do as much work and as quickly as the youngest man on the staff—and to do it better. He rarely misses a day for illness, tells everybody he intends to continue on the job until he "dies in the saddle." He may admit he is slowing down a little physically but not mentally. Age has merely increased his judgment. Fred is usually in the "anti" position at staff conferences —thinks he is exercising a stabilizing influence in management decisions. From his associates' point of view, Fred is a block against new ideas, against taking risks, against doing anything quickly. They have become adept at the art of by-passing Fred whenever possible to bring new ideas into company management—ideas to keep the company in the forefront of their industry.

Fred's company does not have a compulsory retirement policy for executive personnel. It seems, therefore, that Fred will stay on the job until *he* decides he's had enough. Meanwhile, he makes the same decisions he made twenty years ago—except that they become firmer and more authoritative with each passing year.

Aging management people are about the touchiest of all management problems. Should they be compelled to retire? Should there be a uniform retirement age? Should there be any exceptions? Are there adequate pension arrangements for executives? Should the company do anything about counseling for retirement? There is much heated debate on both sides of every such question, and few companies have as yet come up with satisfactory solutions.

Essentially, the difficulty is that each aging manager produces a problem which is as individual as he is—and therefore any general policy which a company may set up would work fine for one man, pinch terrifically in the case of another.

Take the question of compulsory retirement. Companies which favor it argue such a policy is the only way to clear away executive deadwood, open up the channels for promotion, without having to hurt an individual executive with a specific suggestion that he has outworn his usefulness. Given strict enforcement, the policy itself will tend to acclimate executives to the prospect of retirement, provide a painless punctuation to their working careers.

Opponents of compulsory retirement have equally persuasive arguments. They point to the unconscionable waste of scarce managerial talent—seasoned talent, at that—which occurs by indiscriminate shelving of healthy, energetic, productive executives. Further, individual executives vary so much in their capacities, is it even remotely possible to set a uniform dividing line, on one side of which all executives are assets, on the other side of which they are drags upon the organization? Chronological age is never a true measure of a man's capabilities, at either end of the age scale.

Apart from these considerations, what about the appalling personal problems involved in forced retirement? How many aging executives regard retirement as a death sentence somewhat delayed —because of the wealth of reports about executives who have died within a year or two after they retired? How many are worried about money problems?

There are no "answers" to any of these questions. But companies are beginning to explore possible solutions. Many have set up retirement policy, sometimes compulsory, sometimes voluntary, in connection with pension plans for executive personnel. Although such plans have existed for many years in some companies, they have operated more or less on a hit-or-miss basis. Companies felt executives could provide for their own retirement income. Therefore, pension ceilings were imposed, and at a relatively low point. Age limits were generally ignored in individual cases in order to keep badly needed, effective executives on the active list. In the past several years, however, there has been growing recognition that these policies of the past must be up-dated. Taxes and inflation have wreaked havoc with executives' retirement income, have kept men from stepping down even when they wanted or needed to retire. The companies have been making special arrangements in such cases, but would obviously like to be rid of such painful, recurring problems. Therefore, many companies have started to raise or eliminate limits on pensions for executives. Others have been getting around the problem by instituting stock options, annuities, deferred compensation plans. Many companies, large and small, side-step the whole problem by letting executives solve their own retirement problems without a pension—they simply let them stay on the job, either with or without an "official" retirement. If the man "retires," for example, he is simply rehired immediately as a consultant, so-called, usually doing the exact same work.

However a company solves the questions of compulsory vs. voluntary retirement, pensions, counseling, the basic problem is still the human one: few executives are willing to stop working. And few companies are willing to barge in and insist on retirement in the face of resistance.

LOWEST PER CAPITA PAYROLL!

He's Not Human

Philip Downs is manager of the largest branch office of a well-established national company. He received the promotion on the strength of his excellent performance in smaller branch offices of the company, where he had the reputation of having the lowest per capita payroll within the company.

Upon assuming his new position, Phil took inventory of the branch. The first thing his arithmetic told him was that the branch was overstaffed. Without taking time to learn the capabilities or limitations of his personnel, he immediately began to pare the payroll—starting with the people in the higher brackets salarywise.

His next step was to get rid of employees who were potential troublemakers. The records told him that a stenographer on his staff was absent occasionally because of a chronic appendix. She might some day cost the company money if surgery was required. She was terminated under the guise of retrenchment. One of the men had a peptic ulcer which caused him to "go slow" on certain days. He too was released. Neither employee was replaced, nor were several others who also found themselves without employment for "good and sufficient" reasons known only to Phil. It was explained to the rest of the staff that the branch must "carry its weight" within the organization or everyone's job would be in jeopardy.

Phil now had a low per-capita payroll, and his first consideration was to keep it that way. Raises soon became few and far between. He lost some men, replaced them with others at lower salaries. Those who remained were shackled to their jobs by the years of service they had given the company—upon which were predicated valuable pension and group insurance rights which could not be taken lightly. With them on the job, the departments continued to operate more or less adequately and the work got done.

Phil's company was very satisfied with the businesslike job which Phil had done in reorganizing the branch and with his results. He was informed that he was in line for further promotion when the opportunity arose.

The company was measuring Phil's performance on one factor only: his success in reducing costs in his branch while apparently maintaining the same service as before. Actually, the company's management people should have known that Phil's performance could not be measured on that factor alone—or in fact on any tangible factor.

If a top-management man who knew what the branch office should be doing and how it should be operating were to investigate actual operations under Phil's control, he would have found that the office was inadequately staffed and that employees were inadequately paid. This was of course affecting their morale, which in turn was reflected in their job performance. Probing a bit further, the management man would have found that the actual operating costs of the branch in relation to the type of service it was rendering were actually three times operating costs under Phil's predecessor. This was due directly to the inadequate, indifferent, inexperienced, or incompetent manner in which low-priced, demoralized employees were handling their tasks. Actually, therefore, the company was suffering direct financial losses because of Phil's shortsighted and inhuman handling of his people.

Obviously, if the men high in management were interested only in tangibles, Phil was doing a bang-up job by reducing his payroll by so many employees and so many dollars.

BACKWORK!

From Big Piles He Makes Little Piles

Tom Shaw is a tall, mild-mannered man. He walks and sits always slightly hunched over, talks softly and without emphasis, stares at the world with vague blue eyes. He displays a courtly courtesy to visitors, but his own people dread the violent outbursts with which he invariably responds to any problem.

Tom spends his days behind a desk covered with towering piles of work awaiting his attention. There are more piles on his window ledges, on every chair in his office, even on the floor next to him. The only area that seems free of papers is his "out" box. Although Tom works assiduously, very few papers find their way into the "out" box. Rather, they seem to go from one pile to another pile, from desk to window ledge, to chair, and back to desk. Tom looks at one matter, decides it requires more time than he has at the moment, puts it on pile No. 2. He picks up another matter, finds it needs consultation with someone who is out that day, puts it on pile No. 3. The next matter presents a thorny problem—it goes on the window ledge to be struggled with later. And so it goes all day. In effect, Tom moves papers from one pile to another, never coming to a decision, never handling a matter until the fourth or fifth time he has it under consideration.

Tom's department is consistently behind schedule. His people are tense and rushed. Even his large, easygoing assistant, who is ten times as knowledgeable and able as Tom, finds it impossible to put any order or system into his work. He is constantly being summoned into Tom's office to listen to a tirade on how incompetently this matter was handled, or that matter was handled, and why must Tom do everything himself or it doesn't get done right?

Tom's assistant has, in effect, shrugged his big shoulders and stopped struggling. He acts as a buffer between Tom and the department, pouring oil on troubled waters in both directions, getting the work done almost when no one's looking. He tends more and more to take action on his own wherever possible, accepting philosophically the ensuing storm when Tom reviews the matter.

The department has a fantastic absentee rate ("if in doubt, stay out" seems to be the motto) and, except for a few old-timers, an equally fantastic turnover rate. Tom complains constantly about the inability to get work done with such low-quality personnel who have no interest in anything but their pay checks. And, always, the traffic jam in Tom's office flourishes.

There is at least one Tom in every office—a man who knows his job, knows what should be done, but can't make up his mind to do it—or, in fact, to do anything. So the matters referred to him for decision go from one pile to another pile, are considered and reconsidered. Whenever possible, they are sent on to someone else—for further investigation; for review and recommendations; for correction of minor errors—for anything in fact which will delay the time when Tom must act on them. His shilly-shallying delays the work until the last possible minute—thus requiring superhuman efforts from his subordinates to keep the department on anything remotely resembling a schedule. Everything becomes "rush" because of Tom's indecisiveness.

Can Tom be improved? Probably not—he is in his early fifties, has been in his present position for the past ten years, is obviously not going any further. If he were a younger man, Tom's superior might be able to build up Tom's confidence in himself, help Tom to develop the courage to act on his decisions even though he might make mistakes occasionally. He might be able to teach Tom that his advancement in the company depends not on how well he manages to avoid making mistakes, but on the quality of his positive performance in getting work done. In other words, Tom needs to realize that success depends not on "playing it safe"—but on "sticking his neck out."

Well, what should the company do about Tom? He is far from retirement age, a twenty-year man, a man who really does know his job. If the company decides to keep him on, it can do this: reorganize the functioning of the department so that Tom is no longer responsible for making decisions on how matters are to be handled. Instead, put that decision-making function in a job right below Tom. Thus, Tom would remain as Department Manager, for example—and function as a consultant or adviser. His present assistant should be moved up to a position right under him, with a title of perhaps Executive Department Manager—and function as the decision maker. In actual operation, the assistant would make the decisions and be responsible for them; Tom would be available for technical advice, to tell him the advantages and disadvantages of various available courses of action. Tom would see only those matters, therefore, in which his assistant wants Tom's opinion before deciding what to do.

In effect, by this method, Tom is being "walled off" from the actual operation of the department—but the company retains the benefit of his knowledge and experience.

He Wants to Be Loved

Dan Marshall is an extremely charming, facile person who occupies a top-level executive job in his company. He handles the contact work, speaking regularly at business meetings and luncheons. Dan has numerous friends, is always overjoyed at the opportunity of doing a favor for one of them.

Dan is also a very enthusiastic person. When he hires a man, he always hires a "genius" and he sells the newcomer to others in the organization on that basis. The result is that the co-workers sit back and wait for the newcomer to perform. This situation is further complicated by the fact that Dan spells out only vague and unclarified goals for the man—on the theory that he doesn't want to precondition the man's thinking. His "genius" flounders around without help and without results until Dan loses confidence and patience. Just as the man gets his feet under him and is beginning to produce, Dan decides the man is a failure and he must get rid of him. Dan then gives the man an assignment under the supervision of one of his subordinates, Larry. He tells Larry it is his job to make the man produce. This puts Larry on the spot. The assignment is typically nonpinpointed. Larry did not make the assignment nor choose the person to handle it. Nevertheless, Larry is expected to make the man perform, is held responsible for the results. Dan keeps constant check with Larry on the progress of the assignment, forcing him repeatedly to evaluate the man's performance as unsatisfactory and not producing desired results.

Suddenly, one day, Dan is fed up. He calls the man into his office, tells him he must let him go—the reason: Dan cannot justify keeping the man in view of Larry's extreme dissatisfaction with his work. Dan is extremely sorry, still thinks the man has "the stuff" but in view of Larry's attitude, he can't be kept on Larry's payroll and there is no other place at present for him in the organization. Dan will be glad to furnish any references the man will need.

Dan wants everybody to like him. He cannot bring himself to do anything, however justified, which may jeopardize his reputation as a "sweet guy." His subordinates must take turns in being the "heavies" in the constant human dramas Dan creates by his misguided enthusiasms.

Since Dan is in the upper-management levels, his subordinates must live with his weakness. It costs his company untold amounts in wasted salary, disrupted routines, dissipation of effort of high-priced executive talent.

The only solution would be to abolish *one-man* hiring and firing in the company—provide instead, for a committee to pass on personnel acquisitions or separations. This would help temper some of Dan's more enthusiastic and unlikely decisions. It would also eliminate the need for whipping boys in getting rid of failures.

He Can't Manage His Assistants

Albert Small is a department head who is generally regarded as a crackerjack. He is a technical paragon, knows the work backward and forward, knows just what to expect from his subordinates. He has a razor-sharp mind, coldly logical and analytical. Outwardly, he is easygoing, seems to have all kinds of time to confer with his associates. However, his work is always done and done well—because his work pattern is intense and immensely productive.

Albert always has to be right. He has no respect for other opinions, and in his drive to make others aware of his perfection, he reduces his opponents to absurdity by sheer logic. Since he cares nothing at all about wounded feelings, he runs his department with the twin spurs of unassailable logic and unsoftened sarcasm.

In reviewing the work of his subordinates, for example, he can always be depended upon to find something wrong—a decision made on insufficient data; a course chosen which was not the best under the existing facts; an action not cleared with proper officials. When this happens, perhaps in Bill's case, Albert's fantastic memory comes into play. He can always recall another matter handled by another person in which a similar situation arose. Albert then digs out the file on that other matter and calls Bill in to talk to him. He sits Bill down in his private office and says he would like his opinion on a matter which is puzzling him. (Bill and all the other men under Albert recognize this opening as standard operating procedure to one of Albert's dissection jobs on their own work, and immediately begin to tense up.) Albert then gives Bill the facts of the matter and asks, "What would you do in this case?" Bill gives his answer, submits to cross-examination on various alternative decisions. Albert coaxes Bill along to the answer he wants and then pounces: "Well, if that's what should be done in this type of case, as you've just finished telling me, why didn't you do that in this case which you adroitly mishandled last week?" Bill, of course, has no answer since, almost invariably, a mistake had been made. The rest of the interview is a brilliant monologue by Albert, studded with sparkling sarcasm, on the general theme of the incompetents with whom Albert must contend in trying to run the department at even a basic efficiency level.

Daily repetition of this scene (with each of the subordinates taking his turn in the stocks) has demoralized the workforce completely. The men start each work day with dread and foreboding—"who's going to get it today?" In an effort to placate or avoid the sarcastic tongue-lashing, the men approach each problem on their desks with the basic question: "what would *Albert* want done here?"—*not* "what *should* be done here?" Chances of lightning striking seem less imminent if matters are handled this way.

Albert is a fine example of an executive who should not be an executive. He can't be walled off because he would not be happy without someone to beat. He's too brilliant to be kept in the ranks. And he can't be helped except by professionals since the roots of his personality problem lie too deeply. His neurosis shows up only when he reaches a position of authority. He simply can't handle authority in other than a destructive manner which cannot, of course, be permitted in any organization. His domineering, sarcastic manner reduces mediocre men to jellyfish of no use to themselves or the organization. Men of good caliber simply won't stay on.

Albert, the iconoclast, should be released for the good of the company.

DEADLINE !

He Falls Apart under Stress

Reynold Niles is a large-framed, gaunt-faced branch manager; iron gray, close-cropped hair has hidden his youth the past fifteen years. Now, in the mid-forties, he has been looked upon as knowing his business. Three years ago, his boss, Western Division Manager Douns, recounted the history of the company's great and fast nation-wide progress and how the company was relying on Niles to train men for branch managerships in the newer, developing areas.

Since then, the company's growth has advanced at an even faster pace. Douns wonders why Niles has never had any managerial timbre available; he's worried, now, when in retrospect he considers Niles' comments on Dick Grimes, early forties, who looked capable and well and whom Douns had considered for the position he gave Niles; on Jim Rowe who seemed alert and adaptable; on Bob Overmire who picked things up fast and seemed to have good judgment.

During a recent evaluation of these men, Niles mentioned how Dick seemed to be wearing his years poorly. In his forties? Douns remembered that Niles mentioned Dick's back. Didn't he say something about Rowe's heart and Overmire's family troubles giving him a tough time?

The desperate need for fresh managerial talent, trained to the company's ways, in newly developed areas was much too urgent to allow further time to go by. Douns decided to look over Niles with a more critical, discerning eye than ever before.

Niles was a good manager; he got things done, never stayed late nights, had good relations with the company's suppliers, played a good golf game and was the source of much good will for the company. The record was good. But something *must* be wrong.

Douns decided to check upon Dick Grimes' back, Rowe's heart and Overmire's family. His inquiry took him back to the branch office where he found the motivating factors for work by Niles' subordinates to be fear, anger, and anxiety. There was no personal or emotional warmth toward Niles. Papers were found on their desks with notes, all of which ran: "See me—N." They knew that by going in to "see" Niles, they would be reprimanded without ever knowing the real why. Niles would look at them with piercing eyes that challenged them to defy his authority. Niles would press for early action on everything, no matter its relative importance.

Douns remembered his courses in Physics: that pressure and tension can put inanimate matter under stress; that strain was the deformity induced by stress; that elasticity was necessary to recover from such deformation. Douns remembered that elasticity doesn't long last to efficient degree.

By Rowe's physician, Douns was told of an underlying arterial hypertension of only minor extent. Rowe's condition was only a minimal one, without interference with any normal activity, but Rowe's job is not a "normal" one; he is constantly called to a state of emergency by his boss, feels impelled to be *alert* and *ready*; his heart overpumps, his peripheral resistance increases, blood vessels to important organs are seemingly forever constricting, many of the body's mechanisms run short of nourishment, blood becomes sticky, metabolism and fluid balance is disturbed, his head aches, and he begins to hear his heart pounding. Douns went away somewhat confused by medical terms, but he was learning something about stress that didn't come out during his Physics course.

The process of discussion with Grimes and Overmire revealed the great pressure for action exerted by Niles with its resultant fewer informational items collected, assembled, and reassembled; the accumulated stress making for less and less action on less and less adequate information; the likelihood of error becoming greater; the threat of failure increasing; internal strain mounting; backache and family troubles.

The human body as an intricate system of physiological mechanisms is full of unintended booby traps for those made inwardly confused, anxious or uncertain. These physiological mechanisms may become destructive. The setting of specific objectives determines effort, therefore strain, therefore stress. If too many objectives are set for too hurried a pace, the result is an increase over that degree of adaptation to stress situations acquired in the course of normal life. This adaptation is our animate elasticity. Overly employed, it becomes less agile; the ability for adaptation and learning diminishes.

Studies of stress as a factor in general health are minimal in contrast to its tremendous impact on managerial and managerial-potential ranks. On exposure to stress, both physical and emotional (anxiety, anger, fear), a series of reactions take place in the body, in an effort to adapt to the external stimuli which constitute stress. This series of reactions has been given a jargon title by its students, of General Adaptation Syndrome.

In primitive man's struggle for survival, it was necessary to meet external dangers with prompt reactions—a mobilization of all body resources for immediate fight or flight. As a means of commanding quick and efficient sources of energy under such circumstances, there developed mechanisms to meet the sudden demands.

These mechanisms, on appropriate signals from the brain, could produce large quantities of chemical substances capable of transforming body stores into available energy, alertness, etc. These powerful chemical substances circulate through the blood and then quickly dissipate once the emergency has been met. Such body mechanism, therefore, serves a most useful purpose. By students of stress, this has been termed the Alarm Reaction.

Since we have no individual or mass ability to consciously control these complex body mechanisms, they can be set in motion by almost any stressful situation. There is no ability to discriminate as to the significance or importance of the stressful stimulus. Danger and symbols of danger give the same reaction. Eventual depletion of these defensive, protective resources leads to the Diseases of Adaptation (such as hypertension, rheumatoid arthritis, arteriosclerosis, diabetes, allergy, peptic ulcer).

Poor executive performance is vividly demonstrated by those who engender symbols of danger by the transmission to subordinates of their own uncertainty and anxiety. Fear is a fast spreading factor of motivation. It arises and flourishes in the climate of poor communication. Positive group unity can exist only where there is mutual exchange of personal warmth and information. Much has been written and orated on the value of good "climate" in management. When communication breaks down, then the stress and strain in the organization accumulate rapidly.

Chapter IV

Searching Them Out

In our last chapter we saw portraits of men—all of them called executives. We saw areas of conflict; we saw many good reasons why many of them should not be executives. The prevailing attitude toward executives resembles very closely the prevailing attitude toward modern art: "I don't know much about it, but I do know what I like." It is on precisely such subjective and nonarticulated standards that executive performance is being judged.

Ironically, executives themselves are largely responsible. Many of them cherish the belief that there is simply no way to judge whether a man is a good executive. They argue that objective standards for executive performance cannot be formulated because, among other reasons:

1. No two people agree even on the definition of an executive.

2. No two executive jobs are exactly, or even substantially, alike.

3. No two executives operate in the same environment, even within a single company

True. Almost every company defines "executive" according to its own policies, so that a job is executive in one company, nonexecutive in another. But most people will agree that, disregarding artificial distinctions, an executive is a person whose job is getting work done through other people. His job thus necessarily involves a variety and complexity of functions, and so many intangibles that it can't be exactly like any other executive job.

What these arguments prove, however, is only that there is no such being as an "ideal executive." Since every executive job is different, it requires a different combination of qualifications to fill it. Novels, movies and television to the contrary notwithstanding, therefore, executive success is not guaranteed by the possession of certain specified qualities in given specified quantities. A single list of objective standards cannot be formulated for judging *all* executives.

But objective standards *can* be formulated for judging *individual* executives. Take for example Peter Brown, who is being considered for promotion to sales manager. How does his boss decide whether to give Peter a chance at the job? He does it by measuring Peter against the job. Obviously, he has to apply two standards: (a) What skills, experience, personality traits, etc. does the sales manager's job require? (b) Does Peter have enough experience, skills, etc. to be able to handle the job?

Are these objective standards? Only to the extent that they are *applied* objectively. If Peter's boss decides on the basis of a general knowledge of the job and a general impression of Peter, his decision in effect is guesswork—known in the trade as "flying by the seat of the pants." But suppose, while he is considering his decision, he has before him a job profile detailing just what the important functions of the sales manager's job are, what collateral duties he's expected to perform. Suppose, further, he really knows Peter—both his strong and his weak points. Won't his decision, based on this pinpointed information, and illuminated by his judgment and intuition, be as objective as is possible (or desirable, perhaps) for executive posts?

Searching out your bright boys, therefore, requires these two steps:

1. Build up comprehensive job profiles for each management post in terms of the qualities or characteristics needed to have the post well handled.

2. Work up valid and perceptive evaluations of the qualities and characteristics of each of your executives . . . and would-be executives.

By comparing one with the other, you'll quickly see how your men are doing—and why. You'll see which men are in over their heads, trying to do jobs which are too "heavy" for their abilities. You'll see which men are being wasted, piddling around in jobs they can handle with both hands tied. You may even see why these things are happening.

It's a lot of work, let's not kid ourselves. Some of it top management can delegate along the line. But most of it top management will have to do itself. There's no one else who can do it. Is it worthwhile? Take a good look at your organization—then decide.

Profiling Executive Jobs

Before you can pick out your bright boys, you need to know how well they're doing their jobs. And to know that, you need to know *what* their jobs are. Don't laugh. You'd be surprised how many presidents *don't* know—aside from titles—what their executives do. That's why executive selection is such a fascinating game. As generally practiced, it consists of choosing a man with unknown capacities to fill a job with unknown requirements. Think of the delightful possibilities!

For those of us who don't feel playful on this subject, the answer is obvious: executive job profiles.

Who writes them? At last here's something top management can delegate—*after* it draws up a profile of its own job. Obviously, the man holding the job is the best authority on what he does. Let him develop his job profile. But first give him some briefing—incidentally, of course, thus assuring some uniformity in the results.

Have each executive organize his job profile around the same characteristics. Top-level jobs do have certain characteristics in common—despite their wide range of differences. These common characteristics are: Objective, Responsibility, Regular Activities, Rewards, Opportunities. If the executive post is described in terms of these common characteristics, with the differences carefully defined, it becomes possible to compare seemingly different positions, analyze their responsibilities and essential requirements.

1. *Objective.* Every executive job has a particular function, and its first objective is to handle that function satisfactorily . . . manufacture the product, develop sales, provide service, etc. But most executive jobs also have a second function, equally important—to contribute to overall company planning and policy making. The job profile should spell out both objectives, and in detail.

2. *Responsibility.* Each executive job has a certain jurisdiction, covers the activities of certain units or divisions, involves a certain portion of assets, a certain number of employees. The profile should indicate all these and any other factors which will outline the scope of the job. If properly done, this will also spell out the skills, knowledge, experience and personal characteristics which are needed to handle these responsibilities.

Job profiles of responsibility and qualifications usually break down into three main categories:

(a) *General management skills*—skills in planning, organizing, directing, coördinating, handling men.

(b) *Special knowledge or experience*—a broad educational background; enough knowledge and experience in a specialty to be able to supervise the activities of the specialists who report to the executive; experience in responsible jobs not necessarily in the specialty but providing insight into the man's ability to handle an executive job.

(c) *Personal traits*—initiative, vision, drive, ability to formulate plans, judgment, enthusiasm and the ability to instill it in others, emotional stability, decisiveness, and most important, warmth.

One company worked out its job profile on an assistant manager in this form:

RESPONSIBILITIES

Participates with general manager and other assistant managers in development of company policies and programs, long-range planning for improvement of the business and his own department.

Coördinates and directs the activities of Office Manager; General Accountant; Factory Accountant; Manager of Credits, Taxes and Insurance; Manager of Budgets and Planning; Manager of Research and Statistics.

Interprets and applies company policy throughout his organization.

Advises Manager on organization needs and improvements.

Develops plans for his department's operations and delegates execution to his staff.

Counsels and assists his staff in accomplishment of objectives.

Conducts weekly meetings with staff to review performance in relation to plans and objectives, advise on corrective action.

Supervises development and training activities for his staff, with constant check on progress of promotable individuals.

QUALIFICATIONS

College graduate, preferably with major in business administration or accounting.

Five or more years of supervisory experience in positions involving accounting or finance.

Heavy on human relations skills and experience.

Good organizational ability, forceful leadership qualities, good judgment.

Ability to work under constantly changing conditions requiring original thinking, fast action, vision.

Some companies list only the essential requirements of the executive position—those elements which must be present if the job is to be satisfactorily performed. They feel that if the man has at least those qualifications, he should be given a chance at the position. Other companies list every element which they feel the position requires, but indicate broadly which requirements are essential, and to what degree. They then leave it to the discretion of the executive's supervisor to decide whether to give him a chance at the position. In general, the larger companies tend to develop more detailed job profiles because there is less personal contact between the various levels of management and less information as to job content and changes.

3. *Regular activities.*   Some executive jobs deal primarily with objects; others with ideas; others with people. The job profile should pin down the nature and extent of these regular activities. It should indicate whether day-in, day-out activities involve application of standard operating procedures within a set routine—or improvisation and original thinking to meet new situations as they develop. It should indicate the amount of control exercised over the regular activities by the incumbent's superior. To what extent does the incumbent have full authority to act on his own, rather than merely clearing matters with his superior?

Failure to recognize the essential nature of an executive job can mean costly mistakes for the company, painful experiences for its people. For example, one company recently promoted its head bookkeeper to the job of office manager. He had a sound knowledge of the operation of the department, had been his superior's right-hand man for a considerable period. When the superior moved on to a higher job, the man seemed "right" for promotion in every way. However, the company shortly found it had lost an excellent bookkeeper, acquired an inadequate office manager. Apparently, no one had recognized that the man had little talent for working with people, as was very much required in the office manager's job. He had functioned well enough in that capacity as an assistant, who merely transmitted instructions. In the top post, however, he shortly found it difficult to maintain a team spirit, to handle grievances of his women workers, to coördinate the work of different sections, etc. Experience would eventually remedy most of his immediate problems, of course. The company wishes, however, he had acquired that experience piecemeal in the past.

4. *Rewards.*   Some executive jobs pay off primarily in terms of personal recognition or prestige. Others are essentially stepping-stones to better jobs, not rewarding in their job content or job satisfactions but undertaken because of their opportunities. A few

are dead-end, leading nowhere, whose primary reward or job satisfaction is the salary they carry. The job profile should convey this information. It is essential to proper routing of men in view of their personal motivations.

One company made this unnecessary mistake. Its division manager was extremely talented, very ambitious, full of drive and ideas. He was regarded as a promising "comer" by his superiors, who decided to promote him to a position which would add to his background experience in the company. Although a promotion, the job gave him no leeway for self-expression, no opportunity to make mistakes. In essence, the job required him merely to coördinate the work of a small group within clearly defined policies and plans. There were few opportunities for creative thinking within his limited job jurisdiction, and forays into other job jurisdictions were discouraged as a matter of company policy. After the limits of the job became clear to him, the man concluded that he had been placed in a dead-end position because he had reached his ceiling. His performance fell to barely adequate as his self-assurance reeled under the blow. Only after a chance remark by his superior gave him a clue to the reason for the transfer did he begin to regain his confidence. He then set himself to do an outstanding job within the limits imposed. Had the company recognized the result of placing a creative man in a routine job, it could have avoided considerable anguish and self-doubt in a sensitive, gifted individual merely by explaining to him the reason for the move. More importantly, it could have used the transfer as an affirmative means of indicating approval and encouragement merely by proper communication.

5. *Opportunities.*   Some executive jobs provide only a limited scope of experience. After a given length of time, the man has sampled all the situations which the job involves, should have acquired reasonable facility in handling them. Service in the job beyond that point will increase his proficiency, but it will not measurably further the development of his capacities. Recognition of the limited scope of such positions is important to prevent stranding men in such positions.

Most companies set a minimum service period for such jobs, expecting their men to be ready to move on by the end of that time.

Usually, the period is not definitely fixed but remains fairly approximate. Where a man reaches the point of diminishing returns before there is an opening at the next level, he is kept interested by enlarging his area of responsibility with special assignments or addition of temporary duties. Even where an opening develops, his promotion is held up and he is kept in his job for at least the minimum period, if possible. Companies have found that serious morale problems developed where men were moved through the promotion series at their own pace. This problem would not occur in a company where the promotion ladder is not clearly defined, or where there are only a few men at the same promotional level at the same time, rising through different fields, so that comparisons are not obvious, destructive of both individual and team morale.

Written Job Profiles?

Even though the management group is small, it is wise to develop job profiles of executive posts in a written form. There are a number of reasons:

1. *It forces an articulation* (perhaps for the first time) of just what the position involves. Very often no one except the man on the job knows exactly how he spends his time each day. Just as often, he should not be doing some of the things which are taking up his time each day. The trouble is that once a matter becomes part of his responsibility, it rarely leaves him. The reason for the original assignment may long since be gone—but the job remains with him. Looking at the job today, with a fresh viewpoint, and in the context of the current operating scene, it may be very clear that some responsibilities belong elsewhere, while others should be added for more efficient handling.

2. *It may point out the need for reorganization* of some key jobs. A mere listing of the responsibilities being carried by an executive job may be proof complete that the load is impossible for

one man to handle. There is just too much work for one person. But there may not be enough work for two people. However, the same may be true of another executive job. The answer, of course, is obvious: create a third job out of some of the job functions of the original two.

3. *It spotlights objectives.* Frequently the welter of detail which makes up the day's work leaves the executive in the position of "not seeing the forest for the trees." A job profile showing how his responsibilities fit into the overall pattern of the organization may give him an entirely new outlook on what he *ought* to be doing with his time. This in turn will give him a new appreciation of the relative importance of the things he is *actually* doing.

4. *It aids in development.* A proper profile of an executive job could serve almost as a profile of the kind of executive needed to fill it. Used as such, it is a valuable aid in judging the extent of improvement needed and possible in the person holding the job, and in his possible successor. The job profile also helps correct unintentional bias. Frequently, the man in the job tends to concentrate his efforts on those job functions which are most urgent, or which he finds most interesting or challenging. He thus neglects other important areas of the job. The same bias is apt to appear in his activities in developing his subordinates: he naturally emphasizes those parts of the job which he considers most important. The written job profile will serve to give both the executive and his backstop a valuable reorientation in the position "in the round."

After the man in the job has worked up his job profile, most companies ask him to do one thing more: indicate any changes which he thinks would make the position more effective or more satisfying.

Some companies then go further. In addition to a level view of Job A by the man holding it, they try to get backward, sideway, downward and upward views of Job A. They ask the man who previously held the job to write a job profile. They ask the man on the level immediately above to write a profile of Job A. They ask the man on the level immediately below—and the man on the same level who works with the holder of Job A. Do they all agree on the chief responsibilities of the position as described by the incumbent? Do they agree on the most important characteristics the person holding the job should have? Have they any suggestions for changes? The incumbent is asked to consider all the views, develop a final version of his job profile with which he is satisfied.

Now the matter is back in top management's lap. What about those suggestions for changes? Do some of them have merit? Perhaps they point up areas of conflict, overlapping functions, undefined responsibilities—or other organizational distortions discussed in Chapter II. If so, would revamping of some executive jobs correct the situation? After discussion and decision on such points with the executive staff, the job profiles will have to be checked over again in the light of the new organizational setup.

Examples of how a good job profile can pinpoint the kind of man needed to handle the position competently appear on pages 206–07.

The "Good" Executive—Who Is He?

"Good" executives wear different faces. Some of them are forceful, dynamic, extroverted men, who always seem to be hitting on all cylinders. Others are relaxed, easygoing, quietly efficient men, who rarely make a loud noise but somehow keep things moving steadily forward. Both types of men—and all the many types between—are good executives because they are doing a superlative job of meeting the special requirements of their particular management post.

That's the only essential difference between a good executive and an inadequate one. Both men may have substantially similar qualities of leadership, integrity, ability to get along with people, vision, judgment, energy. But one man is in the wrong niche—he's in a job which needs talents he doesn't have, or which needs a different combination of talents than those he has. He's the square peg in the rectangular hole—and both he and the job show the strain.

When the strain is very severe, it's fairly easy to spot poor executive performance—in fact, it would be hard to miss it. Those cases don't present problems of *appraisal* of the executive's work: they involve problems of identifying the *reasons* for his failure. In what specific areas is he falling down? Why? Knowing the reasons for his failure, you will generally know also whether or not he can be helped—even, perhaps, what method to adopt.

The real problem in executive appraisal is to identify the cases where a man is in the wrong job, but is *absorbing the resulting strains*—well enough, in fact, to turn in a satisfactory job. Because he's in the wrong niche, he can't turn in an outstanding job—but this is not apparent and may never be discovered. Instead, the assumption is made that the man has reached his ceiling. Even the man himself may not realize that he has greater potentials. He's too busy making ends meet in his present position. It is in these cases that good executive evaluation can really pay dividends and produce the most dramatic results in terms of preventing waste of valuable managerial talent.

The *good* executive, therefore, is the man who has the talents needed by his job—and who is fully exercising these talents at the maximum of his capacity.

How Do Your Executives Stack Up?

Executive evaluation goes on constantly in every business organization. The performance of management people is being measured against some standard—profits, cost reduction, product improvement, sales quotas, customer relations, whatever. It is on the basis of such appraisals that assignments are routed to certain men rather than to others; that promotions are made; that salary adjustments are determined. The evaluation may be fair and accurate. Or, it may be based on an unrepresentative incident and incorrectly ticket the man. It may have been made prematurely, or based on misleading evidence. Perhaps opportunities did not arise in which the man could prove his abilities and thus revise the original estimate. Sometimes the evaluation itself prevents the occurrence of opportunities for correcting it. Also, and very important, the original evaluation may have been accurate, but the man may have developed in his job, corrected some of his deficiencies—however he's still tagged with the original estimate and overlooked as a possible candidate for higher posts.

Would a formalized procedure for executive appraisal be helpful? Well, it would seem reasonable to say yes. In a company which consciously sets itself the task of taking a fresh look at its people at regular intervals, there should be less chance for executive talent to go unrecognized or for an inaccurate evaluation to "stick." There should be more fairness in the appraisals, since the standards used are defined uniformly and presumably are applied uniformly. There should be less chance of personality conflicts operating to hamper an executive's advancement on his merits. And, since reëvaluations are required at regular intervals, there is at least that much insurance that recognition will be given to improved executive performance.

That's the way it *should* work. Does it? Well, opinions differ. One fact is clear, however; it doesn't work that way automatically. No part of the process of defining executive positions or evaluating executive performance is easy. How could it be? Managerial talent comes in oddly assorted packages. If a company can recognize an executive only when he's six feet tall and wearing a charming manner, its executive evaluations will obviously never disclose the really terrific managerial talent of a man who doesn't happen to be a charming six-footer. No formalized procedure in the world will change that result.

In other words, it isn't the *formalization* of procedures for executive evaluation which is vital . . . it's the *climate* in which the evaluation takes place. In this, as in all other business situations, the only purpose of installing procedures is to provide tools. It is important that the tools be good ones, and that they be used skillfully. It is more important that the users understand that they are only tools—no more.

The brutal truth is that in some of our largest companies, the widely publicized executive development program has never progressed beyond the tooling stage. Elaborate procedures are in operation: executive job profiles are constantly reviewed; appraisals of executives are made every six months on fancy forms; files are being built up on potential executive timbre; all sorts of lovely charts prove how well the executive development program is operating. What does it all mean? It's a wonderful procedure and it operates beautifully. But a procedure for what purpose? Well, they haven't got to that yet. After all, the plan has only been in operation for three years, or five years, or seven years. . . .

It seems it can't be too often emphasized, to even the brightest people, that job profiles and executive appraisals are only basic data to use in deciding how well your executive group stacks up in terms of (a) current performance; and (b) promotability.

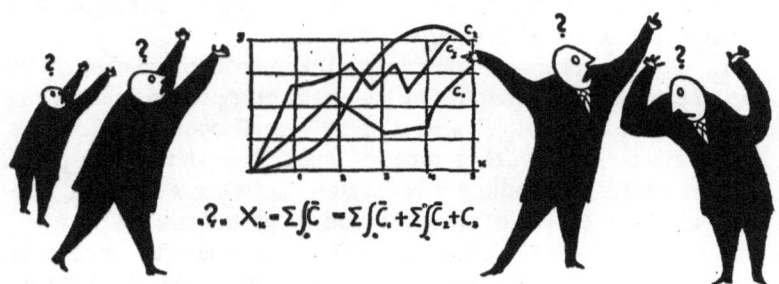

Should You Use an Appraisal Form?

Executive performance can be evaluated without using an appraisal form. You do it every day. But using a form may make the job easier *provided* (a) it's a good form, and (b) it's used properly.

A good appraisal form synthesizes the qualities which you feel your executives must have to do a good job of managing your company. By using the form, all appraisers will be judging management people on the basis of uniform company standards—not on the basis of each appraiser's individual standards. They will also be forced by the form to make their judgments in the context of the man's entire performance, and to weigh them carefully.

Good appraisal forms thus help appraisers measure capacities and limitations in an organized fashion. But they can go further: They can provide a built-in guaranty that they will be used properly. This is accomplished by requiring appraisers to take the necessary second step in proper executive appraisal—measuring the man against his job. Properly constructed appraisal forms will require appraisers to summarize a candidate's qualities into an estimate of how he is fulfilling the essential requirements of his present job—and whether he has potential for advancement beyond his present assignment.

Developing a good evaluation form is understandably not a one-shot proposition. The qualities selected as important, and the techniques for securing estimates of performance and potential, may have to be refined and redefined several times before they really fit the needs of your company. Start off by building the appraisal form around several broad categories, such as:

1. *Job Performance:* measuring the man's knowledge of his job, the quality and quantity of his work, his operating results, his comprehension of the job's relation to overall operations.

2. *Executive Ability:* estimating his skill in developing plans, making decisions, handling subordinates, fostering team spirit, coping with the unexpected, exercising judgment and control.

3. *Intellectual Capacity:* determining the man's capacity to think creatively, analyze situations or problems, distinguish between important and unimportant matters, adapt quickly to the demands of a new situation, understand complicated operations.

4. *Personal Qualities:* evaluating his ability to get along with people, exercise initiative, persevere despite setbacks, overcome discouragements, recognize mistakes and accept correction constructively, develop tact and reliability

5. *Promotion Potential:* measuring the man's ambition, his interest in self-development in terms of his job, his willingness to work for advancement, his patience in learning necessary routines, procedures and policy, his interest in developing improved methods or procedures.

When you have worked out the qualities you consider important to executive success in your organization as well as you can see them now, follow up by asking appraisers to summarize their impressions. Give them room to develop their opinions on specific points. What are this man's outstanding abilities? In what ways does he need to improve? Do you think he rates promotion? How soon will he be ready?

As you work out your appraisal form, keep in mind these suggestions gleaned from the experience of companies who have worked in this area:

1. *Spell out your standards as clearly as you can.* If you merely list the quality you want appraised, each appraiser will be supplying his own definition . . . and the variance may be wide indeed. How much simpler to have the appraisers use your definition. Suppose you want to know about the executive's analytical ability; why not say what you really mean: "Consider his ability to estimate a situation, obtain and evaluate facts, and arrive at a logical conclusion. Does he 'leap without looking'? Does he go off on tangents? Does he miss significant points? Would you be willing to accept his conclusions without checking into them yourself?" When each appraiser rates the man within the same framework, you at least know what information you're getting.

2. *Choose your language carefully.* Avoid generalities, or words that have a vague or indefinite meaning. Don't use words which are ambiguous; or which are frequently misinterpreted; or which carry a connotation, generally or within your organization. Choose words or phrases which are specific, pictorial, simple.

3. *Provide as many shades of evaluation as you need.* You know how meaningless a "good, fair, poor" judgment is in really pinpointing ability. Perhaps it might be more useful for your group to spell out the evaluations in phrases. Suppose you want to appraise an executive's relations with his associates. You might ask your appraisers to check the statement which most nearly approximates the man:

Outstanding in his ability to work with associates.

Works very well with his associates.

Works well with his associates.

Maintains satisfactory relationships with associates.

Has occasional difficulties in working with associates.

Won't or can't work with his associates.

4. *Avoid setting an odd number of evaluations.* Companies have found that appraisers tend to take the easy out, check the middle one. As a result, the appraisal shows the executive as an average, rather than clearly spotlighting his outstanding traits, good and bad. Human nature being what it is, don't use three evaluations, use four; instead of five categories, provide six or eight. If appraisers continue to settle within the middle categories, throw them a curve. Scramble the statements or evaluations so they don't follow a logical progression from "outstanding" to "poor." For example, ask for this evaluation of the quality of an executive's work:

Work usually meets established standards of quality.

Work exceptionally well done.

Occasionally his work falls below standard.

Consistently does a good job on his assignments.

His work is frequently below standard.

Quality of his work fluctuates constantly.

5. *Don't get involved with mathematical scores.* It is meaningless to say a man has 80% score as an executive. Does a 65% score mean he's a failure? Actually, the 65% man may be much more effective in his particular job than the 80% man—or have greater potential. Many companies who used scores have found by experience that they serve no valid purpose in development of men for high-level jobs and have discontinued the practice.

6. *Think twice about using gimmicks.* A number of companies did this when they first began executive evaluation. They anticipated opposition from their executive staff to the appraisal idea, hoped the gadgets or gimmicks would distract attention long enough to get the job done. Some of them used "king-sized" appraisal forms; others included tricky "rate yourself" forms for the executive's private edification (no one else saw them after completion); a few adopted a whimsical approach with "cute" line drawings illustrating the qualities to be appraised, the ratings, etc.

Most of these companies report unsatisfactory results. Even at the lowest management levels, the reaction was overwhelmingly resentment rather than amusement.

As you review the appraisal forms on pages 208–15, you'll notice considerable similarity in the qualities considered important in appraising executive personnel. Don't be misled by this similarity. No one has yet devised a *single* list of executive qualities which a man must have in specified quantities to be successful in an executive post. On the contrary, a man may have all the qualities listed in the various forms and nevertheless perform in a mediocre fashion in an executive job. Ask any president. Top-flight executives do have certain personal qualities in common, apart from the specialized knowledge demanded by their jobs. They all have a drive for achievement, decisiveness, excellent organizational ability, love of activity, strong leadership qualities, adaptability, vision, ability to accept and exercise authority without prejudice. However, executive jobs demand different combinations of these characteristics, place top-heavy emphasis on some, underplay others, depending on the organization. You can't just adopt one of the forms for your own use and consider this part of the job done.

Who Does the Appraising?

The executive's immediate superior is generally considered best qualified to appraise the man's performance. Since he works closely with the man, he is best able to describe his characteristics and job results within the context of the existing environment.

In some companies, the committee appraisal method is preferred. Two or three of the man's superiors meet jointly and go over his performance in the job. The appraisal findings are usually required to be unanimous.

A third approach is favored in some companies. There, apprais-als by two or three people are made of each executive, but no at-tempt is made at having the appraisers coördinate their findings.

Each method has its advantages and its drawbacks. Where one man appraises, his errors of judgment or bias will color the ap-praisal, sometimes with no opportunity by the man being appraised to correct the mistaken review. Where committees meet for ap-praisal, usually one strong character dominates the session and the others string along; or the result obtained may be an *average* rather than a true picture of the man's ability. In some companies, also, there aren't sufficient opportunities for contact to permit two or three superiors to really know the man, be able validly to rate his performance. Where independent appraisals are made, with no coördination of results, appraisals tend to fall flat on their faces. There are bound to be some disagreements. You then have to get an appraiser to appraise the appraisers. The man being reviewed usually gets lost in the shuffle.

Actually, it all gets down to judgment, and most companies pre-fer to accept the judgment of the immediate superior—after briefing him to try to avoid the two most common errors of evaluation:

(1) The "constant error"—the tendency to evaluate con-sistently high or consistently low. Sometimes the supervisor can correct this tendency himself after being shown how his appraisals compare with those of the other supervisors. He can raise or lower his evaluations to bring them in line with the rest of the company. If this can't be done, however, the appraisals made by such su-periors must be gone over by another member of management and revised to correct the rating error.

(2) The "halo error"—the tendency of the person doing the appraising to make his evaluations of each specific factor in ac-cordance with his general impression of the man. Each specific factor is therefore rated good, fair or inadequate, not on considera-tion of the man's performance of *that factor,* but on consideration of the overall impression of performance of the job which the su-perior has already formed.

There is a good technique for handling this type of evaluation error, based on use of a forced-choice questionnaire. The appraiser is presented with several statements describing the man's job performance and is asked to choose the statement which most applies to the employee. The statements are divided into groups of three or four, and are equally attractive to appraisers. Actually, however, they are substantially different in their significance in job performance. The superior thus has to make a selection in each group on the basis of actually describing the man's performance because he doesn't know which statement in the group is most favorable to the man. All the statements in the group appear equally favorable.

To be effective, of course, the forced-choice questionnaire must be developed from within the organization. The method used is to set up 200 or 300 statements descriptive of executive performance. These are submitted to a stratified sample of executives in the company, who rate each of the items in terms of the kind of executive behavior described. A statistical analysis is made of the tabulated results of their ratings, and each statement is assigned a weight according to the extent to which it is used in describing good executive performance. The statements are then grouped into sets of three or four, all sounding equally favorable, but having different significance in measuring executive performance.

An example of a forced-choice questionnaire: pages 216–18.

Appraising the Appraiser

One of the by-products of executive evaluation is that it not only provides a picture of the man being appraised—it provides a picture of the appraiser. An appraiser who grumbles at taking time to evaluate his people is exposing the fact that he doesn't understand one of his major responsibilities. An appraiser whose judgment is way out of line with the actual situation in terms of job performance may be exhibiting bias, favoritism or merely ignorance of what the man is actually doing. If the appraiser comes up with the same evaluation time after time, although in fact the man under review may have improved or grown in knowledge or skill, it indicates the appraiser is hasty, or inept, or just plain lazy—in any event, he is certainly not evaluating the man on his current performance and in light of his current abilities.

All such situations indicate areas in which the appraiser himself needs some development—and companies are finding it useful to use such inaccurate appraisals as a jumping-off point for appraising the appraiser, to help him overcome his deficiencies in this area.

How Much Do You Tell—and When?

After the appraisal, what do you tell the executive? Should he see the appraisal? Here you are in the realm of very human, "human relations," and much depends on the skill with which this phase of the evaluation is conducted.

Most companies insist that an interview take place between appraiser and executive as soon as possible after the appraisal is completed. They advocate frank, open-minded discussion of the executive's performance, the steps he may take to increase his effectiveness. Here are some of the recommendations they give their appraisers:

1.   Before the interview, think about the executive's personality, plan an approach suited to him.

2.   Select a time for discussion when neither you nor the executive is under strain or pressure.

3.   Be sure you have privacy and are not interrupted or over-heard. If possible, arrange matters so that no one else knows the interview concerns the appraisal.

4.   Don't plunge right into the details of his problems. Start on a happy note: talk about his strong points first. Have some nice things to say about them.

5.   When you get to the points on which he needs improvement, avoid at all costs a disciplinary or argumentative tone. Even if you told him the same thing six months ago with no apparent result, tell him again—and say it as though it were the first time and you want to make sure he understands. Don't hesitate to criticize hon-estly—but be constructive. Give him specific details on how he can improve his performance in his weak areas.

6.   Let him talk . . . and when he stops, encourage him to talk some more. Let him tell you how wrong you are in your judg-ments. Listen to what he has on his mind. Answer his questions on how you came to the conclusion that he didn't do this . . . or did that. Don't try to justify your judgments—chances are if he talks enough, you won't have to.

7.   Don't talk about things he can't improve. Such information will not help his current job performance. All it can do is damage his morale—and perhaps permanently.

8.   Don't break off the discussion until you have summarized with him the strong points and the weak ones, come to some agree-ment on plans for improvement. If he needs further education, foi example, you should come prepared with facts on what the com-pany will do to help him meet the costs—or provide time off to at-tend the courses.

How Often Do You Appraise?

Most companies favor six-month intervals between appraisals. They find this is long enough for improvements to occur, not so long that attention is diverted from the objective of developing executives.

An attempt is made in all companies to keep executive appraisal separate and distinct from salary review. Many companies have an established policy that no salary revision will be made at the time of executive evaluation. One disadvantage of annual executive appraisal, for example, is that it tends so easily to become identified with salary considerations. At the top levels of management, however, annual appraisals are customary. The work of executives at this level is so long-range in many aspects that shorter intervals are not feasible.

Some companies establish a three-month interval when executive appraisal is first put into effect. They anticipate that some, at least, of the first appraisals will be unskillfully prepared, want their personnel to get as much experience in evaluation as possible—while at the same time correcting their first unrepresentative judgments.

What about Disagreements?

Suppose the executive disagrees with the appraisal made of his performance? What should the company do? Well, one thing at least is certain: don't try to force him to accept the appraisal. If he and his superior can't agree after a full discussion, it may be sufficient merely to indicate on the appraisal form what the man thinks. In fact, many appraisal forms specifically ask what the man's reaction is to the appraisal.

If the superior at the second level is familiar with the executive's work, it may be possible for the executive and the appraiser to discuss the appraisal with him. Or even better, a new appraisal of the executive may be made by the second-level superior.

Most companies have found that, except in a rare instance here or there, disagreement over appraisal results can usually be resolved in the initial discussion with the executive. If the appraisal

is undertaken in the proper spirit, both men back down a little
and agreement is eventually reached.

Should You Build an Appraisal File?

Definitely not. In fact, you shouldn't keep the current appraisal
after you have discussed it with the man, and plans have been
started to improve problem areas. Next time you appraise, you'll
want to look at him currently and in light of conditions as they
exist then in the organization. The last appraisal is only history.

Appraisals should never "leak"—and where was there a filing
system anywhere which did not have at least one small leak? Even
one such incident could insure that never again would a completely
honest appraisal be made in your organization.

Chapter V

Caution on the
Executive Highway

Your close-up view of your executive staff will give you a new respect for the job they are doing despite their difficulties and problems. The gap between what they *should* be doing and what they *are* doing is now understandable. And as often happens, understanding of a situation carries with it clues for handling it. In every executive problem area, constructive measures will suggest themselves to you. Don't jump headlong into positive action, however. There are some preliminary steps you must take—a foundation you will need before weaving a pattern for executive development in one or more individual instances.

It is implied over and over again in these pages that top management has it within its power to ease—perhaps even solve—many of the problems of its Executive Floor and of its executive staff. All that is needed is acquisition and application of one talent: an informed and sympathetic sensitivity toward its hard-working executive people. This thought can't be repeated too often or stressed too hard. Were it sufficiently prevalent, there would be no need for this chapter—perhaps even for this book.

Go Slow—Create the Right Climate

To the innocent bystander, it often appears that executive development should more aptly be termed executive correction. Although the evaluation of the executive spotlights his strong points as well as his weaknesses, action on the appraisal results is confined entirely to the weaknesses.

It is entirely natural, of course, for the man's first concern to be concentrated on his deficiencies. Everyone wants to be perfect or at least to be considered perfect. For executive personnel, however, this human desire often and mistakenly becomes, in addition, a job requirement. In such an oppressive atmosphere of desired perfection, however, the man will ignore, or put far down on his list, the objective of improving or increasing skills he already has— rather he will devote all his efforts toward eliminating or improving his weak spots.

Such efforts will, of course, render the executive more effective. To that extent, they will benefit the company, but only in the short-term view. Long range, the company may suffer incalculable losses, because its executives waste their time and energy correcting unimportant small weaknesses, instead of concentrating on the task of capitalizing on their strong points.

Frequently, indeed, an executive doesn't have to be outstandingly good to function satisfactorily in his position—it's enough that he's not outstandingly bad. In such subtle ways is mediocrity encouraged.

Creating the right climate, then, may be the most important single step which determines how well executives are developed in your company. Every management person in your organization should be appraising each of his people from the viewpoint of enlarging his capacities, not merely correcting faults. Correction of faults may be a part of the total plan, and an essential part—but only if, and only to the extent that, it is necessarily involved in the broadening of the man's talents. Unless management from the very top down feels this sincerely, no plans will do justice to subordinates' potentials, and will, instead, unconsciously impose an artificial and arbitrary ceiling on development of promising men.

Maintain Speed—Let Well Enough Alone

Not every executive is a candidate for development—and not because he's perfect or because he doesn't have potentials. Some men reach their ceilings prematurely by personal choice. They look at the jobs at higher management levels; calculate their cost in terms of stress, worry, health and other personal sacrifices; and decide: "Not for me, boy. It just isn't worth it. My job is interesting, it pays well enough for my needs, I'll stay where I am." In one company, for example, two division managers have turned down an opportunity for promotion to the home office in the past year—because it involved moving to another state. They decided they didn't want to trade their pleasant suburban living and smoothly running departments for city living and home-office politics.

Sometimes the ceiling is placed on their advancement by factors beyond their control. A man's appearance, for example, may effectively bar him from top management posts—too short, unattractive build, unimposing bearing, pronounced "nationality" features. Such men, despite their technical competence or administrative skill, cannot advance beyond a certain point. Sometimes, the man's name halts his progress, or the college he attended (or didn't attend!), or even his inability to drink large amounts of good alcohol in short periods.

If an executive is not slated for further promotion, there's no point in attempting to develop his capacities beyond the needs of the job he's holding. It is not feasible to develop talents that do not improve his job performance, nor is it necessary to correct weaknesses which don't interfere with his job performance. In this instance, do only what's necessary to make him fully effective in his current job, at whatever level of management that happens to be.

Curve—Recognize the Breaking Point

An executive's shortcomings may be only too apparent—that is, to everyone but him. Before he can be helped, he must first recognize that he needs improvement. Insight and self-analysis are not easily come by, however. Most people require spoon-feeding. This is especially true in the case of the high-strung, sensitive, very bright men who are holding executive jobs. They must be handled carefully when the negative aspects of their appraisals are discussed. If led into too much self-criticism in terms of their personality structure, the evaluation may have disintegrating rather than helpful effects. Most men in supervisory positions recognize which of their men need to be handled carefully in regard to criticism. It would be wise to remember, however, that even men who take correction well in day-to-day work situations may find it difficult to accept criticism growing out of an evaluation of their personality. Their breaking point may be higher, but it's there.

Criticism must be communicated directly and quietly and never through intermediaries, no matter how specially or carefully picked they may be. Such lack of courage displayed by top or near-top management puts unnecessary stress on everybody. The intermediary, if lower in the prestige hierarchy, may experience perplexity, uneasiness, display signs of divided loyalty; if higher in the prestige hierarchy, he may feel impatience, contempt or discouragement. The criticism to be communicated, by inevitable editing en route, becomes distorted and does not have its desired sense, content, or effect. Gossip arises when off the record or confidential comments are made to others about a future member of a management team—with inevitable tension among management, and its resultant collective disturbance involving subordinates. This tension arises from fear of "I'm next." Like infectious agents, fear is contagious—spreading even more rapidly than they do, since there is little or no incubation period for the development of those faculties which warn us of the catastrophe of uncertain performance believed to be poor.

Some men readily admit failures in performance brought to light in the evaluation, but insist the trouble lies not in themselves but in the impossible situation in which they must operate. Occasionally, they're right. Organizational snafus may be bad enough to negate much of their effectiveness. Obviously, no proper evaluation of the executive's performance can be made until a thorough evaluation is first made of his operating environment and its effect on his performance. Very often, however, the primary difficulty is not in the environment, but in the man. On the one hand, he may be creating the environment himself, by his own actions. On the other hand, he may be using a bad setup created by others and may be resisting changes to improve the environment. In either case, of course, his motivations will be obscure to himself—he won't recognize that his actions constitute an effort to hold on to excuses outside of himself for his ineffectiveness. Precipitant action in adjusting the environment may remove the man's psychological supports too abruptly. You'd be improving the environment, not the executive. Instead, it would be wise to work with the man within the existing environment until he, himself, recognizes where the difficulty actually lies.

Some men respond to failure or business frustration with illness.

If you have an executive who suffers from constantly recurring backache, headache or insomnia; irritability; loss of appetite; chronic fatigue; intermittent joint pain or muscular aches; nervous upsets; attacks of stomach or heart pain—for which no organic cause is found—be extra careful in pushing self-analysis or self-criticism. Whether the source of these anxiety symptoms or difficulties is in his home or in his business environment, it takes careful handling not to make matters worse. Many companies are beginning to ask their executive personnel to have periodic medical checkups (including a psychological checkup) to spot latent booby traps. By working closely with their medical consultants, these companies can let the professionals handle those parts of the appraisal in which assistance can be useful.

The Pause That Refreshes

Activities aimed at executive development are necessarily long range. It takes varied and repeated experiences to develop judgment, leadership and assurance. But people need to feel they are accomplishing something as they go along. Although the end results are subjective and intangible, the man needs somehow to measure his progress or development. Otherwise, he may lose interest because he feels he is not achieving anything. In other words, he needs intermediate goals toward which his development is pointed.

One way to meet this need is to give the man specific assignments which can be accomplished in a relatively short period. These assignments can be linked to the man's weak areas, or to his strong ones. As he completes each short-term assignment, his handling of the matter can be reviewed in a coaching interview with his superior. This will give the man a feeling of progress and accomplishment which can carry over to his broader development goals. A man who needs to widen his viewpoint, for example, may find it hard to see if he is making progress. Suppose he works in sales and is assigned to work on a particular project in the production field, such as development of a new manufacturing process. By the time he completes the assignment, he has at least learned something about manufacturing—he has tangibly broadened his viewpoint in that respect. His next assignment may be a project in labor relations—helping to negotiate a new collective bargaining agreement, for example. Establishment of subgoals thus provides a tangible measure for his use and encouragement in accomplishing his overall development program; eliminating tension by activity without sweating it out over an extended period.

Side Road—the Stand-Patters

There are some men who will never enter into the spirit of executive development. Their thoughts and habits are so well intrenched in the self-made office-boy-to-president tradition, they will never change. Such old-line executives rarely respond to education. Good management people may develop in their departments because they are training them in the day-by-day operation of their jobs without being aware that they are doing so. In most cases, however, men who report to such executives are frustrated and thwarted in their efforts to learn more than their current position permits.

If you have such executives in your organization, chances are they are in fairly high positions. In most cases, management development will have to detour around them. Promising men rising through their departments will have to be spotted by other management people, and receive needed experience and skills elsewhere in the organization. Your only consolation is that time will take care of this problem—the new generation of management people is thoroughly sold on the principle that one of its most important management functions is to select, train and develop tomorrow's management team.

We Love Our Children . . .

". . . Don't hurt them." Every executive has some characteristic which annoys the people who work with him. He doesn't pick up his telephone promptly. He talks "through" his pipe. He's always an obligatory ten minutes late for his appointments. He shouts when he gets annoyed. He forgets to consult. He interferes at the critical moment. He begins checking the status of an assignment before the man is fairly out of his office. He tells the same stories over and over.

As his superior reviews an executive's appraisal, he'll note such failings. What should he do about them? The answer will have to depend on how important they are in the light of the man's development—or the development of the men reporting to him. If the man's traits are personality shortcomings, it's generally conceded that the appraiser will have a tough job. His action must depend on the result of his weighing one factor against another. Suppose he's appraising the head of his purchasing department. The man's technical knowledge is excellent, he coöperates well with other department heads, morale in his department is good. However, he's inclined to be too cautious, hesitates to act without confirmation of his judgment, and is always late with his reports. His superior may well decide to concentrate on developing the man's initiative and resourcefulness. He'll tolerate the late reports, not even mention the matter.

Take another case. The sales manager is one of the best teachers of salesmen the company ever had. His analysis of markets, techniques for sales procedures, and ability to work with Production are very good. However, his personality is somewhat brittle and he loses his temper easily and frequently. Pondering this man's appraisal, his superior could hardly hope to change the man's personality. The best he could hope to accomplish would be to make whatever arrangements he could in responsibilities or work-flow to lessen the tension under which the man works. Discussing his temper outbursts with the man would accomplish nothing in view of his personality. So he'll ignore that part of the evaluation, not because it is unimportant, but because he considers it the price the company must pay for a brilliant sales manager.

It's an important consideration. You must pay something for brilliant executives besides money. Sometimes it is tolerance and understanding. Sometimes you don't change the man, you fit the organization around him—because it is this man, and others like him, who make the organization function and prosper.

As you take each person on your executive staff, scan his strong points and his weaknesses, remember you're dealing with people—and with the matters closest to their happiness and well-being. These are people with strong motivation, and with good minds and good hearts, who are beating them to death in behalf of the company. Be careful of their pride; their fears; and, especially, of their dignity.

Chapter VI

Stops along the Way

An executive learns how to be an executive by working in an executive position. There is no substitute for experience. Management skill is developed through trial-and-error in handling the multifarious responsibilities of day-to-day operations. The situations, problems and people with which an administrator deals are never static—they change, react and interrelate with no predictability. There are, therefore, no automatic solutions to administrative problems. An administrator learns how to solve problems and deal with people by making decisions, observing the results, figuring out what went wrong *this* time—and why.

There are a number of techniques by which a company can provide this on-the-job "growing up" experience for its bright people:

1. Day-in, day-out coaching by the man's superior.
2. Making him an assistant to a top executive.
3. Rotating him into different management jobs to diversify his experience.
4. Giving him special assignments or projects.
5. Having him participate in executive conferences and committees.

6.   Giving him public speaking assignments.

7.   Encouraging his active participation in community activities.

8.   Having him become a member of a trade, technical or management group.

9.   Encouraging him to acquire additional education he will need for higher executive posts.

Which method is best? For each executive, the best technique is the one which will supply the knowledge or experience he needs to realize more fully his management potential—to develop himself for better performance in his present job and for advancement to higher jobs. Often a company may use all these methods in varying proportions. The choice depends on feasibility in company operations and usefulness at a particular stage of the executive's development. It grows out of the evaluation of the man's abilities, and is made because it is the best method available at the moment to help the man to increase his effectiveness.

Individual Coaching

Experience in company after company has demonstrated that executives learn by doing—they develop executive abilities best through experience in handling real responsibilities in bona fide job situations. Experience has also shown, however, that *more* skills are developed *more quickly* where the man's superior consciously gives meaning and significance to day-to-day events by counseling and guiding his subordinate. Since the superior is intimately familiar with the man's ability and weaknesses, he can manipulate the working situation into opportunities for increasing those abilities, strengthening those weaknesses. Actual experience in an assignment will teach the executive a certain amount—his superior's objective counseling during and at the completion of the job, will relate that knowledge both to his job requirements and to his personal growth. In a recent survey of sixty-two company presidents, for example, forty-three stated that working under an able executive was the most valuable business experience a person "on the way up" could have toward future success.

Don't confuse coaching with the supervision which exists in every superior-subordinate relationship. Supervision is centered on the *job*—it is concerned with the individual only to the extent of having him use the best method for getting the job done quickly and well. Coaching is centered on the *individual*—it is concerned with the job only to the extent that the individual can extract from it the knowledge and experience needed to develop his capacities. *Coaching starts where supervision stops.*

"What do you think?" A superior who asks his subordinate that question at least once each day is well on his way to becoming a good coach. By drawing out the subordinate's opinion, the superior shows respect for the man's knowledge or skill, thus helping to build his confidence. He may also open up new reservoirs of ideas, even if many of them are neither usable nor practical. If the ideas are not used, the man should be told why. The superior can use the opportunity for emphasizing the need for facts, logical thinking and analysis of the problem. When the man comes up with a good idea, however, he should get full credit. Encourage him to keep thinking by encouraging him to feel free to express himself.

Just two cautions on this method of coaching: *Don't* ask for an opinion if your mind is already made up; *don't* ask for an opinion and then greet it with scorn or ridicule.

How coaching is handled in a large company is explained by one of its executives in this fictional case:

A top executive in the company has a promising subordinate. Evaluation of his abilities has shown that he has one very serious fault which reduces his effectiveness and limits his future—a tendency to make snap judgments. The man's superior, as his coach, has the job of getting the man to recognize his weakness and work on methods for overcoming it. To do this, the superior first evaluates the seriousness of the fault; he tries to determine what is causing it; then he considers various ways of getting the man to see his fault and to accept guidance in remedying it.

"How serious is the fault? The man's snap judgments are based on guesses or opinions. His associates have lost confidence in him because he is so often wrong. His superior hesitates to act on the man's answers until he has done some checking of his own. Under the circumstances, the man is not doing well in his current job. This fault will seriously hamper his advancement to more responsible work. Nothing is more inefficient or tends more to destroy confidence than the correctable bad habit of snap-decisionitis.

"What's causing it? He thinks an executive should have an immediate and definite answer to any question that may arise. He does not realize that a good executive explores problems fully— or as fully as time and evidence permit—before making a decision. He doesn't know his snap judgments have caused trouble in the past—he doesn't investigate the results and no one tells him of his failures. He knows well the specialty through which he rose to his present position and is able to make quick and able decisions in that field. He does not realize, however, that he is ignorant of other areas now under his supervision—and he is applying the same principles to those areas. Also, he hurries too much—he doesn't stop to realize that his present position requires better judgment than lower jobs where he had less responsibility.

"What can I do to help him? First, I want him to see the results of his decisions. I will ask him to draw up a report summarizing his major judgments on various projects in the past year—and their results. Also, I will ask him to join me in conferences with the rest of the staff. There he will see men from other divisions examining and evaluating various reports, including some of his own. This should lead him to question the results he has been so sure of, and the fast judgments responsible for poor results.

"Next, I will have him work closely with me on the problem of a new plant in Oregon. I will ask him to help me decide whether to build now. When he brings me his recommendation, I will ask him whether he has thought of all the factors involved, such as:

1.   Projecting the cash position of the present business somewhat beyond the estimated date of completion of the new building.

2.   Estimating the additional working capital needed to finance the higher volume which will be produced by the new factory.

3.   Determining whether present resources are sufficient to pay for the new factory or whether additional financing is necessary.

4.   Studying the availability and cost of labor both to build and

to operate in the new location, and determining if any employees from our other locations will have to be transferred.

5.   Reviewing and bringing up to date the most recent estimates of building costs.

"I will bring up these and other questions one or two at a time, so he will get the idea of an all-inclusive study himself and, perhaps, recognize his own inadequacy. Each time he reports on any factor, I will question him further to see that it is based on objective evidence, carefully weighed and interpreted. I will arrange to work with him while he goes over some part of his proposal, such as the availability of labor. Then I can see what sources he uses and how he uses them, and perhaps have some constructive suggestions.

"After I have worked with him through one major problem, I will give him several specific problems, asking for his report and recommendations. In each case, I will question him on his decisions until *he* sees the problem as broadly as it should be seen, and until his decision can be squarely supported with facts. When he makes a quick judgment—for example, on the need to alter our retirement plan—and says: 'Everybody is satisfied with it and anyway we don't have enough old people now to be concerned with it,' I will ask him for details such as:

1.   The figures on the various age groupings in our company.

2.   How our retirement plan compares, in detail, with those of our competitors and with other companies in our local area.

3.   What evidence we have, or can get, as to what our people *really* think about the present plan.

4.   The specific costs of various possible revisions of the plan.

5.   What effect such revisions may have on employee morale.

"At various times, when he comes in to report on some project, it is important that I arrange to have other executives present who are well informed on the subject and who hold different opinions from his. Their questioning of him and their own carefully supported cases should help convince him of the need for assembling adequate evidence and giving it careful deliberation.

"I will continue to give him projects emphasizing the need for careful study of the facts and evaluation of various courses of action. Meanwhile, I will comment favorably and strongly as often as possible on some of the senior executives, praising their deliberate, thoughtful and careful approach, and stressing that men at the top use judgment and reflection, not precipitous action.

"After working with him like this for several months, I will review his progress, plan further activities he may need on this or other limitations."

Obviously, the effectiveness of the coaching technique depends almost entirely on the coach. He must have large amounts of patience, human insight and vision. He must be willing to give freely of his time and thought to the process. Most of all, he must be willing to recognize that he himself may be partly at fault in the relationship—by providing a bad example, or being too busy to share his knowledge and experience, or failing to express himself clearly, or refusing to hand over responsibility needed to do a good job, etc. One of the most valuable by-products of good coaching is the measurable increase that results in the effectiveness of the coach himself.

Failure to Coach

An executive's failure to coach his men and help them to grow may be due to a number of reasons, existing in different combinations in individual cases.

1. *The executive may fail to recognize that training of his subordinates is an integral part of his own management function.*

Perhaps this is a reflection of the attitude of his superiors—top management giving lip service only to the goal of developing its people. Or he may be one of the old-line executives who believe a man should pull himself up by his own bootstraps . . . who think that helping subordinates along is coddling and destroys the man's initiative and drive. The man is expected to "sink or swim" on his own merits.

Before this type of executive can do an effective coaching job for the men who report to him, he must be educated himself. He must be made to understand that hard-headed business advantages accrue from a policy of helping men grow up to their potentials more fully. Usually, sad to say, the old-line executive cannot be brought to outstanding performance as a coach. However, he will make conscientious efforts to discharge his responsibilities in this area once he gets the idea . . . and gets it repeated often enough.

2. *The executive may lack time for training.* His excuse is not lack of realization of his responsibility. Rather, he says that there is too much work to get done to spare the time needed to show subordinates how to do the job, then spend more time checking the subordinates' performance. He can do the work himself much more quickly and efficiently.

Such an executive utterly fails to realize that his own efficiency is measured by his success in *getting things done*—not by his success in doing them himself. That is, after all, the function of an executive—to extend his own efforts by utilizing the work of his subordinates to accomplish projects and reach goals. His value lies in selecting able people and so directing their efforts that the work gets done efficiently and well. If he fails to develop such people he, in effect, limits his job, department, or company to a one-man operation.

3. *The executive may be jealous of his position or status.* He makes no effort to help others up the ladder because his primary interest is in his own advancement. He may even fear that brilliant subordinates will pass him by if given the opportunity. He makes sure that his subordinates get no opportunity to outstrip him while under his control.

In such men, thwarted ambition lies at the base of their refusal to help others to grow. Their own performance necessarily suffers because their own potentials are not being realized. It may be wise to investigate the relationship between such an executive and the man to whom *he* reports—frequently the answer may lie there.

Another frequent cause of refusal to coach others is a basic insecurity—the man's lack of confidence in his own abilities, or in his superior's proper evaluation of his abilities. The man's jealous grasp on every detail of his responsibilities grows out of a fear that delegation of even a small part of his job will make his own contribution significantly less valuable. The human relations problem involved in this situation is particularly difficult where the man's abilities *are* limited. His superior must handle the situation with considerable skill and sympathy.

One company which uses job rotation as part of its executive development efforts, reports this incident: men being trained for management posts are assigned in turn to different departments of the business to acquire broad-based experience and working knowledge of the company's operations. There is no specified period set to be spent on any particular assignment. A man is moved along from one department to another as soon as the department head indicates he thinks the man is sufficiently familiar with operations in his department. It became evident as time went on that men were taking a disproportionately long time to "graduate" out of one of the departments. Investigation eventually showed that the head of that department was very effectively holding down the advancement of the men. The department head had reached his top level of promotion and apparently resented the fact that younger men were going ahead of him. He consistently refused to permit the executive trainees to acquire the experience necessary to learn that department's operation. When the department head's superior reviewed the situation, he reported that the department head just did not have the potential to go higher. His opinion was supported by other top-level men who also reviewed the department head's performance. The company solved the immediate problem temporarily by setting a one-year period on assignment of executives to that department.

The department head's superior then began to work on the

problem. First he looked for opportunities in his contacts with the department head to bolster the man's confidence. He arranged for assignment to the department head of special projects in which the man could do an outstanding job, making it a point to give him full credit for his performance. He also looked for opportunities to compliment him on his handling of his responsibilities. Over the course of several months, he gradually brought the department head to accept the fact that he was considered a valuable employee whose contribution was recognized and appreciated. When this was established, his superior then occasionally threw in an assignment which brought the department head beyond his capabilities. When he brought in his report, his superior commented favorably on the parts of the work which were well done, and by questions, indicated those parts which were not satisfactory. The department head gradually realized that he did not have the ability to handle positions with greater responsibilities. However, his superior continued to indicate his entire approval of the man's performance. Thus the man eventually acquired confidence in the security of his position despite his lack of advancement potential. His superior then began to indicate how he could share his knowledge and experience with those under him, thus increasing his own value to the company without in the least impairing his position. The department head eventually made a good adjustment to his status in the company, and his attitude and relations with his subordinates improved immeasurably.

4. *The executive may label parts of his job "confidential."* Since the executive believes that such confidential information should not be in the hands of anyone but himself, he refuses to pass it on to his subordinate. Consequently, the assistant is left in ignorance of whole areas of job functions—to the point, sometimes, where he simply couldn't handle the superior's job should the need arise, although presumably he is being groomed as a backstop.

In small companies, for example, it is usual for one of the key executives to have full charge of sales. He lays out sales territories, handles sales campaigns, sets pricing policies, directs the sales force, etc. Frequently, however, he himself handles the important customers. Only he knows the details of these accounts, such as special handling, discounts, contacts, financing, etc. In most cases, there is no real reason for this secrecy. The executive probably only wants to insure proper handling of the important accounts, and he takes care of them himself because he doesn't want any slip-ups. The net result, however, is that there is no other person in the organization who could step in and manage the accounts if for any reason the executive's services became unavailable. Even where really confidential information is involved, there should be at least one other person who is familiar with the details.

5. *The executive may be "unable" to teach.* He excuses his failure to develop his subordinates on the ground that he doesn't know how to go about it. Sometimes a little probing into the situation will disclose that this excuse is given where the subordinate has personality problems. The executive is reluctant to involve himself in such "personal" matters, feels that it is a matter for specialists to handle.

Occasionally situations arise which do require the services of specialists. They are relatively rare, however. In the majority of cases, the situation merely requires some understanding and sympathetic handling by the superior. Perhaps his subordinate is not aware of the trait or action which is undesirable. Recognition alone may be enough—a newly promoted man who is throwing his weight around may need only a friendly hint on how *not* to exercise authority—given at the right moment.

In one company, for example, the assistant to a key executive was a bright fellow with a lot on the ball. The difficulty was that he knew it, and irritated people to the point of open hostility by his aggressive and superior manner and attitude. The man's insensitivity made it improbable that a subtle hint would penetrate. His superior decided on a head-on approach. He called the man into his office, shut off his telephone, and gave it to his subordinate "straight." He spoke frankly of the man's attitude and the offense it gave to people around him. He discussed in detail some of the incidents which had annoyed his associates, explaining how the man could have secured the same good results without antagonizing the men with whom he was dealing. It was strong medicine, but the man responded—later even with gratitude. In the months that followed, he began to learn with guidance how to approach his associates with tact and with sensitivity, how to tap their coöperativeness and good will.

In cases where correction of the fault requires a basic change of conduct, however, recognition alone may not be enough—a change of habits is difficult. The man will need a patient and understanding superior who won't be discouraged by an occasional relapse.

In handling personality problems, the coach must, of necessity, draw on all his resources of insight and skill. Counseling is never an easy task and the methods vary greatly. Much depends on timing. An effective coach seems to know by instinct what to do and when. A few casual remarks over lunch or inserted in the course of a business conversation may be the extent of his counseling. It's the timing that makes it effective. Undeniably, it's hard work—but great reward is attached. One practical recompense: a coach who conscientiously applies himself to the task of helping his subordinates to grow inevitably succeeds also in making himself more effective. His own dealings with people improve as his efforts give him a deeper understanding of how human nature works.

6. *The executive may hesitate for fear of an unfavorable response.* He wonders whether the situation won't become worse if he attempts counseling and the man becomes sullen or uncoöperative or argumentative. Or if he views counseling as an invitation to unload his problems onto his superior's shoulders? An executive who fails to coach for this reason needs to realize that if such reactions occur, they are symptoms of the need for coaching rather than excuses for failure to coach. The sullen or argumentative response may be due to the superior's lack of skill. It is only after more skillful efforts are made without success that the coach can reasonably assume that the man genuinely does not wish to improve.

In cases where the subordinate wants answers rather than suggestions on methods, the superior must first exclude the factor of laziness. If that's not the answer, he should look for a way to teach the man to stand on his own feet.

An executive who felt that one of the men reporting to him was leaning on him too heavily for decisions adopted this procedure: he instructed his secretary not to put through calls from that subordinate. Instead, she was to say that he was tied up and would call back when free. This procedure was to be followed regardless of how important or urgent the call was labeled. Several hours later, or perhaps the next day, the executive would return the call. The first few times, the subordinate had held up decisions pending an okay from the executive. Each time, the executive listened to the story, asked the subordinate what ought to be done, and then quietly suggested that he do it, *with no additional advice*. Gradually, the subordinate began to call less frequently, and several times on the call-back, the executive was informed of an incident and told that action had been taken because he was unavailable. During this period, the subordinate made several mistakes in judgment. The executive commended him on taking action, then "incidentally" pointed out why the mistake had been made and how it could be avoided in the future. As a final step, the executive arranged a trip out of town during which he could not be reached, leaving the subordinate in charge. On his return, his secretary informed him that the subordinate had aged several years during his absence but had accepted the responsibility. Thereafter the subordinate was put through immediately when he called—he had learned to distinguish between situations where his own judgment was sufficient and those where he could legitimately seek advice.

Notice how the problem of mistakes was handled. One of the hardest things a coach must learn is to stand by and watch his pupil dig himself into a hole. His job is *not to prevent* the mistake from happening—because this would necessarily involve his stepping in and taking over. Rather, his job is to be available for the post-mortem—to help the man figure out why the patient died. What factors did he overlook? What methods did he fail to employ? Did he misinterpret the facts? Men learn more from their mistakes than they learn from their successes, provided they are helped to probe deeply enough to find the lesson, instead of glossing over the error. The coach is there to make sure the probing is done properly. Unless a man is free to make mistakes, he really doesn't have responsibility, for the two necessarily go together. If the candidate is not able to act on his decision (that is, make mistakes occasionally), he in effect merely gathers data on which someone else takes action. He himself is not being given the opportunity to learn by doing.

Every executive who has responsibility for coaching subordinates should make these resolutions and renew them every day:

1. I will look at every problem on my desk as a possible opportunity for coaching my assistant.

2. I will insist that he look at every problem on his desk as a possible opportunity for counseling *his* assistant.

3. I will assign as many jobs as I can to him and let him do them himself, giving advice only when he is really stuck.

4. I will give him hell for his mistakes but I will let him make them.

5. I will consistently give him assignments which require him to do a little more than he knows he can do.

Assistant-to Positions

An effective way to stimulate the growth of a man's managerial know-how is to assign him to understudy a key executive. Acting as his assistant, the candidate should be permitted to handle as much as possible of the actual work which is the responsibility of the executive. The advantages of this technique are substantial:

1. It relieves the pressure of work on the executive, gives him more time to work at his real management responsibilities of decision-making rather than decision-execution.

2. It gives the assistant a toe hold on more responsible duties, increasing his awareness of the complexity of higher management positions.

3. It promotes delegation of duties by top executives by capitalizing on the natural eagerness of promising assistants to take over more and more demanding duties.

4. It points up constantly to the key men their duty to develop their subordinates, thus strengthening middle management for its ultimate top-management duties.

5. It provides opportunities for promotion of men ready to go up the ladder before top-level jobs are available, thus maintaining their interest and alertness during the hiatus.

6. It reveals specific weaknesses or deficiencies of the assistant when measured against the demands of a responsible job, provides time and opportunity to correct such faults *before* he moves into higher level positions.

This method will be successful to the exact extent of the challenge which the "boss" injects into his assistant's job. The chief disadvantage of the method is that the assistant can so easily settle into his job and become an amiable "yes-man," riding along on the boss' coattail. Frequently, the assistant can't do otherwise, because he's the victim of a domineering boss. Just as frequently, however, the assistant in fact welcomes the situation because it gives him an easy "out," an opportunity to duck trouble or danger by avoiding responsibility.

Whichever reason applies, yes-men are a menace on the executive staff because eventually they become worthless as assistants— any qualities of originality or initiative they may have had atrophy from disuse. More important, the entire executive process is handicapped when it's guided by a one-man brain trust operating without the benefit of constructive criticism.

Consider these possibilities in eliminating yes-manism among your executive assistants:

1. *Pull in your apron strings.* Make it difficult for subordinates to hang on to you. If they need additional information which is available from some other source, or when it's a matter of weathering some minor crisis, force them to stand on their own feet and take it.

2. *Don't "leave them the details"—only.* Many executives

think that's just what assistants are for—to handle the details. And that's of course true. But if that's all you let them do, *ever*, very soon that's all they'll be able to do. By continually limiting their chances to assume responsibility by leaving them nothing but superprecautionary double checking and monotonous routine, you smother personal drive. As one discouraged assistant put it: "All I do is dig up data for my boss to act on. Then I go dig some more." A man can't develop his abilities without a reasonably real challenge to work on.

3. *Keep your opinions under your hat.* A smile, a nod or a frown can tip off your watchful subordinates to your thinking just as clearly as a statement. Particularly in conferences, it is important not to cut off the headwork by making your views known too soon. Make them work up a sweat. They may surprise you *and* themselves.

Don't assume that the "assistant-to" method of developing subordinates is not feasible for you simply because your executive group is small. You can adapt the method to your own organization quite simply by appointing part-time assistants—men who understudy key men as a recognized addition to their regular assignments. The formalization of the understudy status is important, however, because conscious attention to this matter may otherwise be overlooked in the press of daily work.

Job Rotation

Moving a man from one executive position to another in a planned manner, in order to increase his understanding of the business and his ability to make large-scale decisions, is widely practiced. It is especially useful as a development technique for executives where the evaluation of an individual shows:

1. A blind spot in his experience or knowledge.

2. A need for providing new challenges because the man has worked himself into a rut.

3. A need to broaden the man's outlook by moving him outside the area of his specialty.

4. A possibility that the man is not in the field in which he will perform best.

5. A need to keep his work interesting to him while he is sweating out a promotion because no position is available for him.

Typically, the man is moved along roughly horizontal lines, with the deliberate intention of cutting across departmental patterns: from a job as assistant treasurer to one as assistant sales manager, from engineering to production, from manufacturing to labor relations work. The basic theory is that capable men usually have many abilities lying in different fields. These are best developed or improved by providing opportunities in which they can be exercised in a variety of different circumstances on the job. Since most positions essentially present a limited scope, it is possible to provide the needed experience only by occasionally moving men into other jobs, preferably into positions which extend their abilities a little more in each change.

Large companies make extensive use of this technique in building up their management people, particularly in the case of their younger men. An example is a large mail-order house which follows this procedure for training its branch managers. For each trainee, a job rotation schedule is set up, tailored to his individual needs. If he has had extensive selling experience, for example, his schedule will concentrate heavily on providing him with nonselling assignments. One man's schedule might cover a period of 60 to 90 days; another man's schedule may extend two or more years. In each case, the man is expected to carry in full the responsibilities of the job in which he is currently assigned. The schedule rotates the man through all major phases of the branch for which he is being developed, giving him actual productive assignments in all activities in which he has not had adequate experience. The purpose is to broaden his understanding of the way the branch operates, and of the kinds of problems likely to be encountered in each segment of the organization. For a sample training schedule for one of these trainees see page 219.

Job rotation on the scale practiced in large organizations has some serious disadvantages:

1. It is expensive.
2. It upsets established plans and operations.
3. It sends inexperienced men into departments where they cannot function at their top proficiency.
4. It upsets employees by sending them a new boss and with him, new methods and frequently new policies.
5. It raises thorny problems where jobs of differing status are rotated so that seeming demotions are sometimes involved in the assignments.

Companies which are sold on the method insist their experience shows that the advantages far outweigh the disadvantages. The new plant manager or production director can be much more confidently appointed—and almost always is successful—where he has proved himself in a variety of lower-level jobs through rotation. These companies insist that nothing can teach a man the skills and abilities required for top-level management positions as well as actual experience on a job where he participates as a worker, not an observer, and is forced to take responsibility for his actions.

Smaller companies will never find it feasible to adopt job rotation on the scale used by the large companies. For one thing, the small company can't afford to lose an executive's services in his current job for any considerable period of time. For another, the experience gained can be pretty narrow in a small organization in view of the costs involved. Where it is necessary to increase the executive's understanding of other departments of the business, the small company can adapt job rotation to its own needs rather simply. It can continue the executive in his regular job but at the same time ask him to carry part-time responsibilities in another job in the department or area with which he is not familiar. More informally still, it is usually possible in the cohesive management group of the small company for an executive to "sit in" on another job without a specific assignment—taking over when the incumbent is on vacation, handling special assignments, etc.

Make very sure when altering an executive's responsibilities for reasons of development that an explanation is made both to the person involved and to the people with whom he is associated. At least some of your people are bound to interpret an unexplained change as meaning that they are not doing well in their assigned responsibilities. Proceed on the theory that this thought will occur in every case of change. Where criticism is not involved, you owe it to the executive to make this clear, both to him and to the rest of the executive team. If some criticism is involved, however, there is no pat answer. Most companies favor the course of honesty: tell the man the truth but with constructive emphasis and in an atmosphere of "let's work together and solve this." The only exception is the case where nothing can be done to correct the deficiency involved. The majority view is that usually such cases involve executives who are either at or close to their ceiling, and nothing will be gained by underscoring the situation. The man probably knows the score, or will catch on without prompting. In such cases, nothing is said in criticism and the change is usually explained as "for operational reasons."

You must weigh the pros and cons of job rotation as a tool for increasing the overall effectiveness of your management people in the light of your own situation, obviously, and with an eye to the cost and disruption of operations involved. The small company will usually conclude it is most useful in the case of the lower-level executive personnel, and most effective when used in conjunction with other development techniques rather than as the sole training method.

Problem Solving

This method of increasing an executive's management skill is widely used, and in the large as well as the smaller company. It involves giving the executive a specific assignment or problem, designed to force him to acquire the knowledge or skill he will need to accomplish it. The problem may be one in his own department, or it may be one involving several departments. The basic aim is to develop the man's powers of organization and decision in actual work situations. He is on his own in handling the assignment: he must analyze the situation, isolate the underlying problems, gather the facts he needs, work out a solution or recommendation. He must then *sell* his reasoning and proposed solution to his superior.

Company practice varies widely on the margin of error permitted the trainee in these problem situations. Some companies prefer to have the superior step in when the man goes far afield in his attempts to cope with the assignment and wastes too much time. The majority view, however, is that the man should be allowed to learn from his mistakes, rather than be prevented from making them. Accordingly, the superior does not interfere in any way with the methods used by the man in handling his assignment. When he comes in with his report, the superior usually asks him to detail his analysis and conclusions. If the superior sees a mistake or omission, he doesn't tell the subordinate just where he went wrong and why—instead, he tries by questioning to get the subordinate to think further, discover for himself the particular aspects of the problem which he overlooked or evaluated improperly. The subordinate is then asked to review the problem some more, come back after further study and discuss his recommendations again.

The advantages of this management development technique, when employed with sensitivity and care, are substantial:

1. The assignment is real, based on an actual business problem. The executive is therefore productively contributing to the company while improving his grasp of management problems.

2. The assignment can be slanted to the particular deficiencies of skill or knowledge of the man being trained, thus building up his weak points as revealed in his executive appraisal.

3. The assignment can provide real challenge for the man by deliberately extending him beyond his previously proved capacities.

Thus it can prevent him from getting stale on his job, substitute for promotion when jobs are not yet available up the line.

4.   The assignment gives the superior the advantage of the subordinate's specialized and intensive knowledge or experience, or his different point of view—which the superior might otherwise neglect to obtain.

5.   The assignment can be a proving ground for testing men with management potential, deciding whether they are ready for promotion or need further seasoning.

There is an almost unlimited variety of situations in which companies use the problem-solving technique to advantage:

1.   A traffic manager assigned to his assistant the job of making a complete survey of heavy-duty trucks on the market, investigating the experience of other companies, recommending whether the company should continue to use its current truck model or switch to some other model.

2.   An office manager asked his assistant to study the reasons for the high turnover rate in the stenographic pool, suggest possible corrective action.

3.   A department head asked his subordinate to prepare and present the annual report for the department, summarizing the progress made in the past year, outlining plans for the future.

4.   The head of the engineering department of one firm requires each member of his staff to work up a report on some phase of his work, to be presented and discussed at one of the monthly meetings of top executives of the firm.

5.   A sales manager asked each of his three assistants to make an independent study of the sales problems in a particular area, prepare a dealer-training program on how to sell a new product in that area.

6.   An assistant to the vice-president was assigned the project of investigating employee morale, including a critical evaluation of employee opinion surveys, suggestions on improvement of existing communications, recommendations on how to increase human relations know-how of foremen and supervisors.

7.   A labor relations manager asked his assistant to study the labor grievances which had developed in each of the company's

plants in the preceding year, recommend indicated changes in the existing union contract for discussion at the next renegotiation.

8.   A plant manager asked his assistant to investigate the work flow among the various operating departments, try to discover the causes for bottlenecks, work out with the various department heads possible changes to increase efficiency.

One company makes effective use of this technique in testing the management potential of its promising executives. It assigns men who show management talent to active participation in company contests. One such plant-wide contest was held recently, aimed at improving employee performance in five areas: safety, housekeeping, attendance, reduction of scrap, and product improvement. Management people at all levels participated in the contest. The initial planning was done by a steering committee, made up of the older executives and union representatives. This committee established the framework for the project, set up the contest budget. The steering committee then turned over the job of actually running the contest to the younger executives. They were given assignments to working committees and on these committees had a free hand in working out such contest plans as deciding the contest theme, fixing starting and ending dates, awarding prizes, setting up scoring rules, working out publicity stunts, scheduling special events to keep up employee interest. The steering committee was available for advice, but did not participate except as required for the committees to work together efficiently. The younger executives also acted as coaches—one for each of the eighteen teams into which employees were grouped for purposes of competition in the contest. To lead his team successfully, the coach had to get to know each member well, learn the team's problems, help to solve them, and work to keep interest directed toward the contest goals. The coach also had to work with the standing committees, ironing out difficulties which arose as the contest proceeded, because of the make-up or operation of each team. The contest was adjudged a great success in its primary aims—the final *permanent* level of workmanship was measurably higher than it had been before the contest started. The company also listed these gains in its secondary aims:

1.   Younger executives participated in committee work with nearly eighty management men at all levels, received a dramatic lesson in the principles and value of efficient organization.

2.   The younger men were forced to carry responsibility for execution of plans which they themselves had made—whether they proved successful or unsuccessful.

3.   Coaches were deliberately assigned to teams which were far removed from their usual spheres of activity—thus broadening their understanding of company problems, operations and employees.

4.   Coaches received valuable human relations training by their endeavors to build up and maintain a good team spirit among the employees on their teams—as well as by their experience in working out "beefs" with the committees.

5.   Younger executives received valuable training in cost consciousness by being forced to judge their proposed projects for the contest in the light of their available budget.

6.   All management people agreed that the contest was a forcible demonstration that a relaxed boss-employee relationship, an informed employee and a common goal gets results not obtainable by driving methods—in other words, that it is far better to *lead* than to *drive*.

7.   Unsuspected management talent was uncovered in some of the new or younger executives, causing them to be earmarked for further development; several of the young men who worked effectively in previous contests were further tested in the current contest and were found to be ready for additional promotion.

No matter how small your company or your executive group may be, you can make effective and extensive use of the problem solving or special assignment technique entirely within the actual daily operation of your business. Opportunities constantly arise for the executive to call upon the talents of his subordinate, both to aid him in handling responsibilities and as a training exercise for the subordinate. All it takes is conscious and sustained attention to the value of such action. But there are several cautions which should be observed to get full value from this development technique:

1.   DON'T make "tongue-in-cheek" assignments. Give your assistant a practical problem which actually does exist in your organi-

zation, so that he can work on it in the knowledge that his time and efforts are being profitably expended.

2. DON'T short-change him on the benefits he can derive from the assignment by (a) prematurely deciding the issue for him, (b) failing to give him the facilities he needs to gather his facts, (c) placing an unnecessary "rush" on the assignment, or (d) being either not available or too available for guidance.

3. DON'T make the assignment a life-or-death proposition by giving the impression that the man's entire future depends on how well he does with it. The process of developing good men is a life-long one. Give the assignment its proper value within that context.

4. DON'T hold the reins too tightly. Let him stumble around on his own if necessary, even though it *is* time consuming and unnecessary in your judgment. You'll get much valuable information about the man's capacities and attitudes from the kind of mistakes he makes, and the manner in which he handles them. So will he!

5. DON'T abandon the assignment in midstream. When the man comes in with his report or recommendations, listen carefully and sincerely. Question him on his methods of analyzing the situation, collecting the evidence on which he bases his conclusions. Discuss the pros and cons as fully as possible. When action is finally decided upon, let him know the reasons for the decision, how the various possibilities were weighed. Remember that the result of his efforts is important to him in helping him evaluate the kind of job he did.

6. DON'T be afraid to make the assignment tough. The point is to force the man to extend himself beyond what he already knows he can do. Although most of the assignments will probably fall into more-or-less familiar areas, deliberately throw him one occasionally which will require him to expand his horizons—and don't forget to be constructive if he falls on his face.

Conferences

Many companies use conferences to develop their management people. There is wide dissimilarity, however, in what is meant by

conferences as a development technique. Some of the more common activities embraced by this term are:

1. *"Sitting-in" on conferences of top-level executives.* This
method is usually employed for men at the next lower level of
management who would not normally be included as members of
the conference. One or two of these lower-level executives are invited to attend the weekly or biweekly sessions at which company
problems or plans are discussed. If there are more than a few such
lower-level executives, their invitations are rotated so that the conference does not get too large for effective action. Usually, the
invitees are asked to participate in the discussions whenever they
feel they have something to contribute.

This method is very valuable where the conference involves a
problem-solving or plan-making group. The invitee can learn much
from watching top-level executives analyze the situations before
them, weigh the various alternatives open to them, and decide the
action to be taken. In addition, he secures valuable information on
the manner in which the business is actually operated. If the atmosphere at these conferences is such that the invitee actually does
participate, freely and deeply, this development technique is un-
equaled in benefits.

But there's another side to the picture. In some companies, the
conference is not really a conference at all. It is merely a convenient method for the top executive to impart his decisions to the
group. The men don't meet to work out plans or solutions—they
meet only to record their objections, if any, to a course of action
already decided upon. It is sometimes possible to change the top
executive's decision, but the whole emphasis is on approving or
disapproving a decision he has already reached, rather than on considering facts and reaching a group decision. Such conferences may
be useful in teaching a lower-level executive how to get along with
the top brass, but they certainly don't aid in the growth of the executive's analytical ability, judgment or scope. A lower-level executive
(or a higher-level executive, for that matter) would be rash indeed
to put himself on the spot by attempting to persuade the top brass
to adopt a different course of action.

2. *Attending in-plant training conferences.* Most of the larger

companies use this technique extensively for their new or low-level management people. The conferences are conducted on the company premises by a conference leader and are aimed at imparting knowledge or skill needed by the participants to meet the responsibilities of their executive jobs. The conference leader attempts to get the group to find solutions for their actual work problems by group discussion and sharing of experiences.

Although this technique is employed widely, there is as yet no definite evidence of how effective it really is in developing management qualities. Some companies report considerable success—others have found it disappointing. Such information as is available indicates that this technique, like most others, cannot be used as the sole development device for upper-level people. But it can be very effective as an additional method. Analysis of the experience of companies using the technique indicates these cautions, if effective results are to be obtained:

(a) *Avoid interruptions.* Hold the conference at the office only if you can arrange complete privacy. You must separate the men mentally, as well as physically, from their jobs and their desks. If they will be harried with "important" telephone calls or similar urgent messages if the conference is held on company premises, then by all means hold the conference outside—at a nearby hotel perhaps. Some companies go further: They hold the conferences at an entirely different locality, so that the man will not be tempted to drop in at the office in the morning or in the afternoon before the conference starts. The point is to have the man concentrate completely on the subject of the conference without distraction from his job—so that he can go back to his job with new vision, maybe even a new method of handling his job problems.

(b) *Use a conference leader.* Particularly with your upper level personnel, time is important and short. Giving each man actual practice in conference leadership, by having him take a turn at leading the discussion, results in an awkward pace. A trained conference leader can cover the ground better and quicker. For those executives who need or want training in conference leadership, the skill can be taught at a meeting for that specific purpose.

(c) *Keep the conferences short.* Most companies hold sessions for a one-week period, repeated perhaps at three-month intervals. Experience has shown that many men can be away from their desks for a week at a time without serious bottlenecks or backlogs—but longer periods work a considerable hardship.

(d) *Keep the group small.* Most companies limit the group to from nine to twelve men. Smaller groups tend to get bogged down in more detail than is necessary. Larger groups tend to stray away to side issues.

(e) *Keep the group mixed.* Experience shows that at least three levels of management should be present at each conference —more where the management group is relatively small. Be careful that the highest-level executive present doesn't dominate the group, however subtly. If possible, have at least two management people at the same level at each conference.

(f) *Vary the techniques.* In a typical conference, there is usually a lecture or exposition of the topic under discussion by one or more speakers. This comes early in the day, usually at the beginning of the morning session. Questions and comments from the group follow the presentation, after which the group goes into a round-table type of discussion, reducing the material presented to concrete problems or situations. The conference leader should be able to throw out for discussion some actual cases in the company's experience if the group has none of its own to hash over. The conference should not be permitted to remain strictly a lecture.

Audio-visual aids are very useful in presenting information to the group. These can include diagrams, charts, photographs, films or recordings. They can give the members of the conference more complete and precise understanding of what is being discussed, maintain their interest. Much of this material must be "homemade" to be sharply focused on the current issues or problems in which the group is involved. Experience has shown that these aids are most effective when they can be kept simple and presented slowly so that the men can assimilate the exhibit quickly and easily and then return their attention to the speaker. Many conference leaders like to have a large blackboard or scratch pad always available—use it to jot down key phrases or outline the main points of the topic being discussed.

A technique which is increasingly used in conference training is role-playing. This involves setting up a typical problem in inter-personal relations—then asking two or three members of the group to act out the situation spontaneously. The rest of the group observe the pattern of behavior which develops. When the portrayal is fin-ished, the actors are first asked to comment on their own handling of the situation. This gives each actor the opportunity to criticize himself before the audience is allowed to comment. Such face-sav-ing is especially important at the start of the conferences when the participants tend to feel awkward and hesitant about participating. After the actors have said what they wish, the audience is then en-couraged to comment on their reactions. Sometimes the same situa-tion is played over again—but with the actors reversed in their roles and not limited by the previous pattern.

The advantages of role-playing are many. It is one of the best methods yet worked out for getting the men involved in a problem to recreate the actual situations giving them trouble. The individual may state his problem to the group quite objectively, but the situa-tion may appear entirely different when he has acted it out and demonstrated the procedure he used. When he has received the ad-vice of the group on his role-playing, he will have a much more concrete understanding of how he could conduct himself more ef-fectively in a similar situation in the future. Role-playing thus can change the man's attitude—something which is less likely from a mere intellectual or verbal discussion of a case. Role-playing also helps the man gain insight into his own behavior—particularly where the role-playing is recorded, and the man can listen to a play-back later and judge his own performance as a member of the audience rather than as an actor. Role-playing has the further ad-vantage of presenting actual opportunities for the men to practice and develop skills—thus making it easier to apply those skills in "real life" situations.

But role-playing as a conference technique also has disad-vantages. It requires that the group be approximately at the same status level. Senior men do not like to take the parts, and their presence as observers puts junior men under considerable stress. Further, their remarks can be very discouraging. Also the conference leader must be trained in the role-playing method, able to relieve any player who begins to founder so that the experience will not prove unduly embarrassing or discouraging. At the start, at least, this will usually require that the leader be secured from outside the company. Later, of course, men can be specifically trained in the technique.

(g) *Use outside speakers.* Most companies find this is best since it promotes freedom of comment, challenge and discussion. The group may hesitate to tear into the speaker or question his comments if they have to "live with him" later. Such delicacy usually doesn't extend to executives from other companies, or to university personnel. Outside speakers are also advisable for smaller companies who may lack persons on their staff able to handle such assignments, and who especially need to get outside viewpoints, information or techniques.

(h) *Do some advance "propaganda."* Before the conferences start, brief the persons who will be attending on what topics are to be discussed, try to get preconference interest and participation.

One company started by deciding that conferences should cover five management fundamentals: planning, organization, staffing, controls and leadership. Before scheduling any conferences, the company distributed a statement of these topics to the executives who were to attend the conferences. It asked them to think about the topics, consider the points within each area which they thought should be covered. A week later, it sent each executive a list of questions aimed at further provoking his interest and thought:

. . . How can you and your staff be trained in the planning and leading of discussions to get your problem solved with the advice of the group and in a reasonable time?

. . . How would you proceed if you were developing a long-range plan for expanding your part of the business?

. . . How can you do a better job of keeping up to date on your major functions so that you would have more time to think ahead and continue activities aimed at your personal growth?

. . . Do you think you have adequate control over your people . . . or too much?

(i) *Keep the discussions practical.* Your first few sessions will necessarily cover fundamentals, and will be rather broad and general. But as soon as possible get to a tie-in with the company's actual operations and with the executives' actual responsibilities.

One company which is using the conference technique has worked out its program into four one-week sessions. The first week's unit deals with the general principles of management. The other three weeks are devoted to discussions of the specialized functions of each of the company's divisions or departments. Topics covered include financial administration, manufacturing and engineering, marketing (including advertising and sales), personnel administration, public relations, purchasing, research, traffic. The discussions include lectures, visual aids and problem solving. In addition, conference members are taken on visits to the various departments of the company to see at first-hand the situations discussed in the conference.

(j) *Follow up.* Don't make the mistake of thinking that development of management talent is a once-over proposition which can be disposed of in a classroom or at a conference. Usually, the first conference presents executives with so many novel concepts and ideas that it would be impossible to get the full benefit of each of the lectures at a first meeting. The first conference will produce discernible results—some changes in attitude, beginnings of a broader view of problems, and for some men, an increased efficiency in their day-to-day operations. Equally as important, the first round of conferences will pique the interest of the participants so that at least a few of them will look actively for assistance on some of the problems which they now recognize for the first time. Keep this interest alive and flourishing. One way is by a follow-up conference six months or a year later. The men will come to the second conference with different attitudes and certainly with different problems. The second conference will thus be quite different from the first, even though the same people are participating and the same general topics are under discussion.

The smaller company will usually find it advisable to use a different schedule of meetings than the one-week sessions advocated by large companies. Not enough of its management people can be spared for a week at a time where the management group is small.

A solution worked out by one small company is to have a one- or two-day preliminary meeting during which the basic principles are hammered out. Almost every company can spare its top and middle-management people for a day or two. The conferences thereafter are held at intervals of two weeks, for one day at a time, with none of the participants permitted to miss a meeting because of pressure of work. Another solution is to have the conference meeting start in the late afternoon and run into the evening. Most companies will find it possible to work out an acceptable schedule if enough interest is aroused in the participants so that temporary inconveniences will be disregarded.

3. *Attending outside training conferences.* These conferences are usually arranged by universities or management associations and involve intensive study of all the various phases of one topic. Some of the conferences are aimed at top-level management people—others are designed for middle-management executives. Typically, the conferences start with talks by one or two experts in the field under discussion, after which the conference participants are invited to ask questions, explore the problems being discussed.

These outside conferences are very useful, especially for the smaller company, because it exposes the executive to contact with business and professional experts he could not otherwise consult. Many of the speakers at such conferences are top-level executives who share the benefits of their experience with the group. In addition to the actual knowledge imparted, the small company executive has the opportunity of broadening his acquaintance among executives of other companies, both at his own level and above.

Small companies will find it advantageous to combine outside and in-plant conference training. This is true, for example, where the executive group is small, or where some men have had previous conference training while others have not. Executives who need or want knowledge on the basic principles of management first attend a conference held by a university or management association. After they acquire this preliminary indoctrination, they and the other management people can proceed to the in-plant conferences which in such cases will be concerned almost entirely with material geared to the company's specialized problems. Another advantage of having some executive attend the outside conferences is to insure that the group is kept abreast of new techniques or new material which may be developed out of the experience of other companies.

It will be necessary to do a certain amount of research before training conferences can be started. Most companies find it best to place one executive in charge of the project. He can check material available from colleges or universities, books, management associations, etc. From this, he can develop an outline for the conference program. Special material dealing with the company's individual problems will be secured from within the company, naturally. Usually, each department or division head is asked to make a report from which a stranger could get a comprehensive picture of how the department or division operates. The material thus secured is then pruned down as necessary to fit the requirements of the group and the time available.

Many companies find it useful to develop conference manuals where experience shows that the conference method has proved beneficial in developing their executives. Again, such a project is usually assigned to one executive. He secures samples of such manuals from other companies or from management associations, develops his own along the same lines. The manual is then used both as a training device in itself and as a guide to the conferences.

Back to School

Business firms are increasingly taking advantage of university-level programs designed to assist in executive development. These programs vary widely but all are aimed at helping businessmen become more effective all-around managers. Some are designed specifically for top-level executives; others concentrate on specific problems and are designed for men at lower operating levels of management.

Generally, the university programs fall into three types: (a) a lecture series, which an executive can attend on a day basis and in which he has no homework; these usually run from two to three days at a stretch, (b) courses which the executive can attend at night, which may carry homework but which do not interfere with his job; these usually run for about two or three hours a week per course per semester, and (c) full-time, live-in programs which run about two or three months at a stretch, take the man away from his job for the period of the program.

Obviously every company has to make its own decision on the value and feasibility of such outside educational courses for members of its management staff. The smaller company may well find it difficult to spare an executive from his job for any extended period of time, thus ruling out the live-in, full-time program unless the executive is willing to participate during his vacation. The cost of such programs is another factor which may limit the choice available to the smaller company. The employer usually foots the bill for these courses, as well as continuing the man's salary while he's attending them.

Caution: The usefulness of the outside educational course is largely dependent on how well it ties in with the man's actual job experience. There's no point, for example, in providing a man with a course aimed at giving him a viewpoint about human relations in management—if that viewpoint is in fact at variance with the attitude in operation in his own organization. Nor is there much to be gained from sending him to learn how to formulate top-level policy, set up administrative procedures, evaluate results—when the best he can hope to accomplish in his company is to act as errand boy to the president. Such divergence between what should be and what is can't be cured by sending executives to school. The bright ones will take the education—and put it into effect elsewhere. The lazy ones will go to the course (better than working, a break in the routine), listen cynically, retain nothing. The dull ones will take copious notes, make tremendous reports, and reassure top management that it is keeping up with progressive companies in executive development techniques—without in the least disturbing the existing routines. This is exactly what is happening in too many companies who boast about their gaily packaged, much documented (and wholly ineffective) "executive development program."

These courses *may* be of some aid to your executive candidate. They cannot and will not *make* a good candidate, or *make* an executive for you. Only you, and those who, by working for you, have exhibited the attitude, work habits and loyalty which make you select them as executive candidates, by working together tirelessly and enthusiastically, can develop executives.

The best-known and most emulated of the educational programs for executives is that offered by Harvard University in its Graduate School of Business Administration. Called the Advanced Management Program, it consists of an intensive course of study for mature, experienced executives. It requires full-time attendance for twelve and one-half weeks, is intended only for men who are expected to climb in their company without any ceilings on their advancement. No specific background or formal training is required, the main consideration being whether the man has demonstrated in his business career that he has outstanding qualities of ability, leadership and adaptability. The man must be nominated by top management of his company. He is then further screened by an Admissions Committee which tries to get in each class as wide a diversity of business experience as possible. There are two sessions each year.

The formal study program covers six major areas: (1) Business Policy—covers policy making and administration at the top-management level, (2) Administrative Practices—permits members of the course to exchange experiences in administrative problems arising in relationships with people in business organizations, (3) Business and the American Society—examines social and economic forces which influence policy decisions of administrators, (4) Cost and Financial Administration—studies administrative use of accounting data and budget procedures as an aid to management control, (5) Marketing Administration—developing understanding of problems of marketing and sales people, and (6) Problems in Labor Relations—analyzes trade unions and patterns of labor-management relationships.

Classes meet six days a week—typically number about 160 men from approximately 140 companies. There are guest speakers, but the lecture form is deëmphasized in favor of case studies of actual business situations which are obtained from business, labor and government administrators.

The companies are expected to pay the salaries of the men while they attend the course and provide for their tuition and living expenses. Tuition currently is $1,000 plus a medical fee of $18.75. Dormitory accommodations range from $235–285 per person for the whole course—and men are encouraged to use dormitory accommodations for the "cross-fertilization of ideas" which results from afterhour associations. Meal charges run $500–700 for the whole course, and dues for extracurricular activities average about $100 per student.

The Harvard program is aimed at men in their forties who are on their way up. The average age is 44, age range of the group is from 36 to 55 years. Average length of business experience of a student is from 15 to 20 years. The program tries through its case studies to broaden the attitudes and scope of the men attending. Under guidance, the men learn to examine their habits of thinking and feeling, discover and eradicate biases, faulty thought patterns and undesirable personal traits. The instructors take the attitude that there is no one answer to the problem or case history under discussion. They do not even indicate which solutions are desirable—leaving it to the students to decide from the discussion what methods are most useful in various situations.

Men who attended the last sessions included: General Auditor, General Purchasing Agent, Vice-President, Production Manager, Treasurer and Director, General Sales Manager, Comptroller, Director of Industrial Relations, Director of Management Planning, Auditor, Plant Manager, Claim Director, Research Director, Director of Laboratories, Assistant to President, Retail Sales Manager, Division Supervisor.

The Harvard program has been extensively, though less ambitiously, copied by colleges and universities throughout the country. Even their announcements of their executive development programs are strongly reminiscent of Harvard's brochure, down to the idiom employed. Many of these brochures, in fact, are so well-packaged they rival the best "art" of the best advertising agencies in the business. Despite the purple prose employed, however, it is still too early to evaluate the usefulness of the courses in terms of job behavior of the students. This much is certain, however, and would be no matter how conservatively packaged the courses were: the courses can only be a tool in the development of executive talent. The best *school* for executives is still on-the-job training in the real-life situations with which they must cope successfully

To give you a bird's-eye view of what is available in outside schooling for executive-level personnel, some of the other courses are described on pages 227–42.

Chapter VII

Taking Stock

You've been looking at (and to a certain extent into) your management people, trying to identify the solid ones, help them along in their individual patterns of growth. You've started the wheels moving. But in which direction?

Your objective is clear enough . . . an effective, hard-hitting executive in every management post who is handling his present job well, while at the same time he is enthusiastically preparing himself to take on a more responsible job in the future. There will then be an orderly flow of management-trained, management-minded executives moving up through the various levels of authority, ready to step in and carry on efficiently whenever an executive position becomes vacant.

But how do you gear the development activities of your individual executives to your overall objective? Obviously, they must be tied in together. You will undoubtedly experience personal satisfaction from your efforts to promote the growth of your subordinates. But to serve the interests of your company, you must make sure that the growth you are promoting is channeled to your company's future needs for management people.

In other words, the developmental activities of your individual executives should be plotted out in the light of your company's specific requirements, both short-term and long-range.

Projecting Your Executive Needs

Activities in developing your management people will necessarily proceed in a kind of vacuum (as indeed they do in far too many companies) until you come up with answers to questions like these:

1.   Do we have all the management positions we need in order to operate efficiently in the immediate future?

2.   If not, which positions must be created—and when?

3.   Are all management positions being handled satisfactorily? If not, when is action necessary?

4.   Are there any positions which may need to be filled in the next year or two because of retirement, a health problem, etc.?

5.   Are there any plans under consideration (merger, building a new plant, moving to another state, entering a new business field) which may increase or decrease our executive requirements —or affect the kind of executive we need?

6.   What executive manpower do we have—in kind and quantity?

7.   Do we have the people we need to fill our present management spots?

8.   If not, do we have time to develop one of our own people to take over the vacant spot? Or must we go outside for a qualified man?

9.   Are we running too close to the bone? Too few people at our executive levels?

10.   If we must bring in new people, at which management levels should they come in—in order to be most beneficial to the organization?

Trying to answer these and other similar questions requires you to project your company's needs for management people into future years. Obviously, this involves evaluation of both the company's and your executives' growth potential; inspired guessing about economic developments, not only in your industry but in related businesses; constant revision and up-dating of plans and decisions as events make your company's future needs more discernible. It's a lot of work. Is it really necessary? Well, stop and consider for a moment. Aren't you already doing this same kind of long-range forecasting in every other area of your business? Don't these considerations determine your decisions on production scheduling? sales campaigns? purchase of materials? modernization of plant or equipment? addition of new product lines?

Actually, therefore, you are now being asked only to extend your existing methods of forecasting and planning to solve another important problem of your business: continued successful management.

Diagraming Your Executive Needs

The easiest way to visualize what's going on at the management levels of your company is to map out an organizational chart. Your sales manager needs only a glance at his sales map to know where salesman Brown is currently assigned, how his sales compare with those of the other salesmen. Your production manager can look at his production schedule and spot for you not only the section which is having difficulty, but the conditions which created or contributed to the problem. An organizational chart is the same kind of tool as the sales map or the production schedule. It gives top management fingertip knowledge of the assignment and performance of each member of management.

The chart shows all existing management positions and their relation to each other within the organizational structure of the company. It also indicates who is filling each position; how well he is handling his job; whether he is qualified for further promotion, and when; whether organizational or promotional gaps exist, and where; in what areas action must be taken, and within what period.

The information on the chart is a synthesis of the judgments formed in evaluation of the executives, plus the top-level decisions made on the basis of those judgments. The chart is therefore revised as often as new judgments and new decisions are made. It is not considered a promotion guide—few companies believe a man should be groomed to take over a particular position, except at the highest levels. The chart is used only as a sort of "inventory control" in the execution of long-range plans for the movement of executive personnel.

A word of caution: many companies have organization charts which look terrific on paper—period. The chart has no relation at all to what is actually going on in the company. In effect, the chart represents the *ideal* model, rather than the *working* model, of the organization. Remember that this chart is meant to be a tool for top management's use in developing the executives the company needs. It should represent facts, not hopes.

Organizational charts may be complicated or relatively simple, depending on the structure of the companies they are intended to represent, and the detail of information which is shown. For samples, see pages 220–25.

How's It Going?

Evolving plans for the growth of individual executives, and providing the developmental activities they need, is fine. But don't stop there. What about results?

It is at this point that many of the elaborately packaged management development programs now in existence fall on their well-publicized faces. Don't be misled by the drivel put forth in some quarters about the inability to measure results in this "highly sensitive field."

Of course you can measure results. Executive ability may be an intangible—but its results are all too tangible. And these results are either improving or they're not.

What you should *not* do is expect too much—to look for dramatic improvement in results too soon. In an individual case here or there, the removal of a personal or organizational block may trigger just such a swift and fabulous transformation. Usually, however, the man's growth, as reflected in his results, will be slow, achieved with difficulty, subject to occasional setbacks. Your span for measurement should be months, rather than weeks, in most cases. Your standards should be flexible, applied with understanding and sympathy.

How should you check on progress? Depends on what you're checking. Where the technique you are using is coaching, for example, the superior in effect checks results every day as he watches the man's development in day-to-day operations. The same is true where an executive has been placed in another job temporarily to diversify his experience. But where a man is given a special assignment, chances are his superior will let him go at his own speed, check only at natural "breaks"—as when the man comes in for advice or when he reports on work already completed in the assignment.

In other words, evaluation of development activities, and whether they are producing the desired results, must be done constantly and currently in the light of day-to-day developments. Unless this is done, the wheels may turn but nothing is happening.

Some companies like the idea of formal follow-up interviews, in addition to the day-to-day observation. Depending on circumstances, they schedule these follow-up interviews about once a month. At that time, the superior and the executive talk over the current status of his performance in the light of his individual problems. The follow-up interview, these companies feel, serves as a check for the man on the progress of his development—something his superior might overlook where the man's progress is satisfactory.

Normally, the man's superior handles the follow-up evaluation. If there are difficulties, or if it seems useful to get another viewpoint, he may ask another superior to sit in with him on one of the follow-up interviews. These matters are handled very informally in all companies, the criterion being only what seems advisable at the moment for the executive's best interest.

What about Smaller Companies?

Does the smaller company need to involve itself in organization charts? With only a few management levels and a small group of executives, is it worth-while for it to set up the machinery of organizational charts, executive inventories, etc.?

That question comes up again and again, in various forms, at every stage of discussion of the methods by which a company can help its management people to grow. True, the smaller company can recognize its management problems among those discussed in Chapter II. It can recognize some of its management people in the gallery examined in Chapter III. But the smaller company somehow feels there ought to be short cuts it can use to develop its people—simply because it *isn't* big or wealthy.

Actually, the smaller company's difficulties are not with charts or forms as such—it has cheerfully borrowed and adapted most of the business methods and procedures pioneered by the large companies. Management of the small company is always alert to a *better* way to inventory materials, or a *faster* way to process sales, or a *cheaper* way to handle shipments—and it isn't at all bashful about accepting these improved methods simply because they originated in some large company.

So it isn't the organizational chart or any other form which impels top management of the smaller company to hang back. The difficulty is far more basic. Precisely because the executive group *is* small, and the levels of management few, most of the preliminary analysis of company operations and evaluation of executives will fall squarely on the shoulders of top management of the smaller company. What's even more disturbing, since practically all of the executives report directly to top management, top management itself must plan and put into effect the developmental activities each executive needs to develop his management potential. The prospect appalls the two or three men who typically constitute top management of the smaller company—each of whom is already wearing four or five "hats."

Is it really that bad? Or is it possible (as has happened in many companies) that the investment of time and thought by top management in preliminary analysis of the company's organization and operations will start paying dividends immediately? Can this happen, perhaps, because the analysis:

1. Spotlights areas of responsibility which top management should delegate to near-top management?

2. Indicates areas of responsibility which can be assigned wholly

to one top management person—rather than receiving the attention of the entire top management group?

3.   Eliminates double-checking or other unnecessary and time-wasting controls by top management?

4.   Suggests possible reassignment of responsibilities among the top management group to consolidate related activities, provide quicker action?

5.   Discloses unsuspected blocks to communication among members of top management—or between them and other management people?

In other words, it boils down to this: Every company—large, smaller or small—must take the same steps. Each must analyze its organization, evaluate its people, decide in each case what its people need to develop their management potential. The large company has more work to do at each step; also more people to help with the work. The smaller company has less work to do at each step; also fewer people to do the work. Both can get the work done better and faster by proper use of tools (forms, controls, techniques), adapted as necessary to individual circumstances.

Evaluation Controls

Many companies feel it is desirable to have some sort of control by the department head or manager over individual executive development activities. The department manager is expected to keep himself posted on the progress of each management person in his department, even though the actual development technique is in the hands of the man's immediate superior. By doing so, he can spot superiors who are falling down on their job of developing their men—jack them up immediately. Without this control, individual executives might be retarded in their progress because of a superior's ineptness or lack of interest.

Some companies use forms for evaluation control which are very simple, and the details of which can be handled by the manager's secretary:

1. The first form is a sort of timetable showing that evaluation, follow-up interviews and reappraisals are being completed for each management man. The manager's secretary keeps this record up-to-date, jogs procrastinating superiors. She refers to the manager only those cases in which she can't get coöperation. The department head or manager can see at a glance which superiors are not giving proper attention to their development duties. Such a form is valuable for the department head even though it measures the performance of superiors in only one aspect of their development duties, the aspect most easily subject to review. It is meaningless, for example, to count the number of coaching interviews the superior has had with his subordinate—it's not the quantity but the quality of such interviews which is important. However, checking on whether the superior has evaluated his subordinate, and is following up the evaluation, does have significance for the department head—even though by negative implication. The fact that the superior conscientiously evaluates and reviews doesn't necessarily mean that he's doing a good job in developing his subordinate's management potentials. He may be, or he may not be—all the form indicates is that he's at least paying lip service to his developmental job. However, the fact that the superior fails to evaluate and review *is* significant—he clearly is not giving even lip service to his development duties. This first form could be a chart showing:

> Job Title and Name
> Initial Interview
> 1st Review
> 2nd Review
> 3rd Review
> 4th Review
> Evaluation Completed
> Reappraisal Due

2. The second form is a report on the man's progress. It is filled in by the man's superior after each interview and discusses his de-

velopment activities, how well they are working, whether there has been noticeable change in the man's attitude or characteristics, whether changes in the techniques employed might be profitable. At the top of this chart list (a) the name of the developer, (b) date of initial interview, (c) person being developed, and (d) present position. Under this, with space for comments and date, record:

> Recommended Program of Development
> 1st Review
> 2nd Review
> 3rd Review
> 4th Review

With this information, the department head or manager can keep a running check on how development of his executive is progressing. Periodically, perhaps about every three months, the department head can meet with the superiors for a general discussion of development activities at that point. These meetings give superiors a chance to exchange their views on techniques and effective methods of using job situations to develop management skills. The department head gets a chance in these meetings to indicate improvements in coaching or evaluating which might be useful in individual cases.

With periodic reviews of this sort, development can proceed in an organized manner, with emphasis shifted as may be indicated in a particular case.

In an organization where such close attention is given to management development, it's fairly certain that management people will be given a chance to develop their full potentials. Also, the educated guesses which have to be made concerning future executive needs of the organization will probably hew quite closely to the mark. Most important, the executive in such a company can really believe that his need for challenge and upward progress is recognized and encouraged by an understanding top management.

Chapter VIII

Making Them Work Together

Civilization has taught us that an individual can achieve results through group action which are impossible to achieve by his own efforts. Whether it's playing baseball or running a railroad, you won't succeed unless you can obtain the help of other people who will work together as a team.

But to work together effectively, people must have direction—they need someone to coördinate their activities, channel their efforts toward the common goal. That is management's job. It is the most delicate and the most complicated of all the functions which management performs.

To understand the true dimensions of this function, consider its various aspects:

1. Top management must set the goals toward which the organization is working—and translate them into objectives which are desirable to the members of the organization, at the various levels.

2. Top management must coördinate its own activities (unless it's a one-man top management) in terms of both present and future operations.

3.   Top management must direct and coördinate the activities of the management team.

4.   Top management must direct, through the management team, the activities of the entire work force.

5.   The management team must coördinate its activities in line with the objectives and policies set by top management.

6.   Each executive must direct and coördinate the activities of the departments for which he carries responsibility.

7.   Each executive must direct and motivate the people who report to him.

8.   Each executive must integrate his activities with those of the other members of the management team.

Effective execution of these and the countless other ramifications of this management function turn in essence upon two factors: *communication* and *motivation*. People at all levels must know what they are expected to do, must have adequate information on which to act. In addition, they must *want* to act, and to act in coöperation with others. Good communication plus adequate motivation will equal good teamwork—a smoothly operating, effective organization.

Management's Role in Communication

The importance of good business communication has been increasingly stressed in recent years—and has correspondingly become increasingly stressful upon management. As one top-flight executive put it:

This year, the so-called answer to all our management problems is good communication. All we have to do (so we're told) to insure successful operation of our business is to learn to write good reports, give good speeches, hold good conferences. Some of our boys are having their difficulties—but I tell them not to worry about it so much. If they can just hold on, next year they'll be given another so-called answer to all our problems. And maybe, next year, *they* might make the genius of industry roster.

He's got a point. It's easy to go overboard on the subject of communication. It's easy because there is so much confusion over just what management should do about communication.

Ask a management person if he's satisfied with communication in his company and he'll typically answer something like this: "It's pretty good, by and large, but we're not very satisfied with our employee publication." When you ask why not, he'll tell you that "it doesn't look very interesting"; or "it always seems to sound the same"; or "it gets tougher and tougher to find material"; or "no one wants to work on it." If you were to continue your questioning, you would find that the executive's thinking is concentrated entirely on the problem of how to "spark up" the publication.

Here is a typical example of misdirected management attention to communication. By preoccupation with the details and minutiae of communication procedures, management tends to overlook its real function in this area. Actually, it's the job of the specialists on the staff to execute the procedures. It's the editor's job, for example, to "spark up" the publication. Management's attention should be focused rather on the underlying policy decision involved. Does the unsatisfactory publication indicate a need to reëvaluate the original management decision that communication in the company would best be accomplished by using an employee publication? Would another method of communication be more suitable? or perhaps a combination of several methods?

Management's function in communication—as indeed in all other areas which are legitimately management's concern—is to provide effective planning. In this case, of course, the plans would be aimed at maximum utilization of communication to achieve the company's goals. In other words, management attention should be directed to:

1. Articulating the subjects on which it should initiate communication.

2. Handling its own communication with skill and with dispatch.

3. Analyzing the various factors in the company from the viewpoint of choosing the methods of communication best suited to its circumstances.

4. Setting up channels for communication upward and side-ward—and keeping them in use.

5. Evaluating the effectiveness of communication in the company, at all levels, on a continuing basis.

How Much Communication?

The trend in most companies is toward near-total disclosure of operating information to management people. The feeling is that the more executives know about the company's operations, the better will be their decisions. Therefore, they are kept informed of the company's current operating status, the outlook for operations on both the short-range and long-range basis, plans being evolved in various areas which may affect their decisions.

On policy matters, there is more variance. Executives in some companies participate in setting of policy to a very restricted extent, with only the top two or three levels actively consulted. Executives at the other levels are informed of policy after it has been set, but still with no information on the reasons for the policy. Other companies, however, look upon policy information in the same way as operating information, give as much information as is available to their management people.

What Is Good Communication?

Good communication starts with top management. In some companies, the whole problem of communication would be 90% solved merely by securing acceptance of this fact by top management. Obviously there must be complete awareness of the purposes of management—each executive must understand his status in the structure of management and the meaning of such status. Conflicts must be resolved by open discussion; otherwise serious strain will exist because of the uncertainty created. This uncertainty increases the individual's anxiety, and if prolonged, leads to disorganization of the group by producing an overflow of confused and contradictory messages.

Good communication lessens anxiety and uncertainty in one or more members of the group by neither ignoring them, nor supplying further confusions and contradictions. Instead, it will demonstrate respect for the anxious one's feelings, provide an explanation of or a reassurance about the matter causing difficulty, provide evidence that the group does not share the man's uncertainty.

Good communication is as varied as the many types of business activity. It may be technical, it may be literary, it may be written or oral, but it shares these common characteristics:

1. There is a correlation between the content and the form of communication; any variation in the content of the message goes together with the variation in the form.

2. The networks employed are informal.

3. These communication networks are flexible and subject to alteration whenever need arises. Tension is liable to arise when the opportunity for change is blocked by too rigid red tape. Expectations must be set tentatively, not rigidly; subject to later correction. This flexibility implies the correction of expectations as well as versatility in action.

4. An optimum balance between official and unofficial channels is maintained.

5. Rumors and trial balloons are never employed. They yield no useful effect; create unnecessary tension and uncertainty.

6. The content is real—not calculated to disguise or deceive. Recently a company which by long custom provided a Christmas bonus told its employees that the bonus "would not be given this year." It offered the explanation that the company had lost considerably in one of its operations. Management double-dealing was

clearly evident to any employee with mathematical skill sufficient to perform the simple arithmetic of adding up profits made by the company in investments and in other operations. This company lost employee respect as well as management potential by not stating its *actual* reasons for denying the expected bonus. Such tactics destroy morale, create a basic distrust in further management communication.

7. People are made to use communication procedures properly and routinely.

8. There is good coördination so that executives get only the information they need to make decisions—not information about everything that's going on. They haven't time for unnecessary communication, and each piece of information which comes to them requires action on their part—if only to make sure the proper person gets it.

What Kind of Communication?

Almost all companies use a combination of oral and written communication. On operating information, for example, written communication is usually employed as more convenient. It typically is passed on to executives on a monthly basis as current operating statistics are compiled, perhaps in the form of a "Letter from the President," and includes:

1. Analysis of the previous month's operations—sales, cost of sales, profits earned before taxes, earnings per share.

2. Analysis of inventories—historical comparisons, plant and warehouse figures on an increase/decrease basis; breakdowns of raw materials, goods in process, finished inventory; probable future levels.

3. Industrial relations developments—turnover figures, personnel plans, policy changes, new work rules, information on union relations.

4. Purchasing notes and plans.

5. Public relations developments—information about the company to be contained in future news releases, advertisements, speeches to be given by company officials, appearances before trade associations, radio or television appearances.

6. Engineering and research notes—new products under development, changes in operations which are under consideration, changes in product design or packaging.

7. Major personnel changes to be put into effect in the immediate future.

Communication on policy is done more often on an oral basis—in meetings or conferences with management personnel. The feeling is that there is less chance for distortion or misunderstanding where policy is transmitted face-to-face. Executives have a chance to ask clarifying questions, and the answers are uniform for the whole group.

Lateral Communication

In most companies, communication upward and downward is fairly well systematized. Everyone knows what information to give to whom, when and how. The problem is in lateral communication—or communication between people at the same level. When the pressure goes on, executives just don't get around to passing along to each other information which will be helpful in keeping operations going forward smoothly. As a result, two or three executives may do the same thing independently—or none of them may do it at all. Either there is too much communication—several people getting the same information and all acting on it—or there is not enough communication—no one getting the information. The reason is that when problems multiply, there is a tendency on the part of executives to look even more closely to their contacts up and down. But it seems okay to "postpone" seeing the executive next door until later—and later more often than not never arrives.

Although the result of pressure, this lack of horizontal communication is also a major cause of pressure. The executive in this situation remains uninformed of developments outside his department which directly affect him. He fails to adjust his operations to those of other departments, solves problems already solved elsewhere, makes decisions he has to change later on, and in general— "has to work like hell to catch up with himself later on."

Two executives who found this problem impeding the operation of their management team have attacked it this way. One man has persuaded the president of his company to schedule an executive luncheon once a week, which all members of the management group must attend, no excuses accepted. Information gets exchanged at these luncheons with few slip-ups. The second executive has his secretary remind him daily to spend at least 15 minutes with one of the five men on his level. Should the meeting be postponed, she carries the debt forward and doesn't leave the executive alone until he's discharged it.

When Communication Breaks Down

In some companies, the management team works smoothly, effectively. In others, it seems to hurtle from one crisis to another. What makes the difference? Very often, it is simply poor communication. An organization runs on communication, of necessity. People need information to do their jobs. The information must be accurate and well coördinated. It must flow not only up and down, but laterally between departments. It must go to the people who need the information, and it must go to them on time.

When communications break down, members of the management team find themselves making decisions which later have to be revised in the light of information available but not considered by them when the original decision was made. Why wasn't it considered?

1. Someone forgot to inform an executive. Is it clear that the executive should get the information? Is it clear how he should get it? Would it be helpful to set up a routine procedure to feed him such information in the future?

2. Someone assumed he had been informed by another source. Are there two or more channels of communication for the same information? Should a single method be instituted by which the executive will be kept informed?

3. The executive was informed orally and forgot. One company has set up this slogan in strategic locations: "Write it down—then we'll both know it."

4. The executive misunderstood the information. Did that happen because the communication was ambiguous or unclear? Was the important information "buried" in a long report he didn't have time to digest completely? Did he receive it when he was hurried, or distracted by a pressing problem?

In some organizations, communication flows along the proper networks, but at an almost imperceptible rate of speed. By the time it arrives at its destination, it is more properly categorized as history rather than as current information. There is no real breakdown in the communication process—it just takes too long. Solving this problem may be tougher, actually, than is the case of the breakdown, because there's no obvious place to start. Tracing along the communication network, you may find a bottleneck—a man who is so busy he doesn't get his reports out on time, or who holds them up waiting for "final" figures, or who prefers to let reports accumulate and then get at them all at once. His attitude reflects his lack of understanding of the use to which his reports are put— or of their importance in feeding higher management current information which helps it evaluate past policies, adjust current plans, formulate future decisions. Such lack of understanding may be surprisingly widespread, especially in the middle or lower-management levels where the men have not had the opportunity of participating in executive conferences and seeing the importance of good communication to effective management.

What Makes the Team Work?

Assume your communication setup is working fine. Your management people understand their place in the organization structure, receive the information they need to make good decisions and take proper action. They know what information they should be passing on to others, and along what channels their communications should travel. They know and do all these things. But somehow the communication is not acted upon properly. For one reason or another, action is delayed, or not coördinated with related activities, or just not taken. Obviously, it's not enough for your people to know what to do, they must *want* to do it.

What motivates your management people, makes them want to take action, work as members of a team? The fact that they find deep satisfactions and rewards in being part of the management team—such deep satisfactions, in fact, that they willingly and enthusiastically put forth every effort to insure the success of the team and their continuance on the team. These rewards won't be the same for each member of the team, since they are rooted in the man's personality. It is top management's job to discover in each case the combination of satisfactions which the man is seeking, and to provide them to the fullest extent possible in his job.

But why top management's job? We're dealing with executives—can't we expect them to have insight into their psychic needs and ability to manipulate their tasks to satisfy these needs? Unfortunately, a man's I.Q. has no relation to his self-knowledge. It is still management's nondelegatable function to sense the man's emotional requirements from his job, try to see that they are fulfilled.

But suppose that top management has done this—and still the management team doesn't seem to work together. Conflicts between members occur regularly enough to keep the whole team off-balance. It might be helpful in such cases to look into the possibility that subgroups within the management team may be exerting the disintegrating influences.

Effect of Subgroups

Within even the smallest management team, there may be a number of subgroups composed of some of the members of the team who share a common interest not shared to the same extent by the rest of the team. Some members of the team may belong to only one of the subgroups, or they may belong to several. For example, your management team may contain some or all of these typical subgroups:

Members of the "original" management team

Men who attended the same college

Men who belong to the same social group

Men who are vice-presidents

Men who "came up" through Production (or Sales or Engineering)

Men who are on first-name terms with the top management group

Men who regularly lunch together.

Members of these subgroups are influenced in their attitudes and actions not only by the individual members of the group, but by the group itself. And if they belong to several subgroups, their actions are influenced to some degree by each of the subgroups.

How does the group act upon its members? Well, first you must consider how cohesive the group is—how strong its attraction is for its members. If the attraction is strong, the influence of the group upon its members will also be strong because members will strongly want to "belong." When a difference of opinion arises in the group, some members will take extreme positions for or against; the rest will be neutral, more or less, taking positions about in the middle. Pressure will be put upon the extremists to conform—and the more cohesive the group, the stronger will be the pressure and the more effective. The extremists will have to conform or leave the group.

For example, take the executive committee of a publishing company, which consists of four men. This is a very cohesive group, naturally, and "belonging" is very important to each of the members. They are considering the advisability of publishing a certain manuscript. Editor A is completely in favor of publication, Editor B completely opposed to publication. The other two editors see arguments for and against, are in favor of publication after certain revisions are made. How will the "group" behavior rules affect the decision? First, Editor A will try very hard to convince Editor B that he's wrong—and Editor B will try very hard to convert Editor A to his viewpoint. Neither will succeed, of course. Meanwhile, great pressure is put upon both A and B to conform to the views of C and D. Both A and B try hard to convince each other because they have a common interest which is vital to them both, namely the success of the business. However, when neither can persuade the other, each is faced with a choice: continue in his extreme position, or conform to the pressure to compromise. Since each wants to continue to belong to the group, each will conform to the pressure, and modify his position. The final decision, therefore, will be similar to that advocated by C and D, the middle-of-the-roaders.

The result will be different, however, if the group has a low cohesiveness. In that case, when neither A nor B will change his position, the group will disintegrate. The pressure upon A and B is not strong enough to force them to compromise because neither cares very much whether or not he continues in the group.

Even a highly cohesive group can disintegrate when its pressure upon its members is vitiated by the greater pressure of a subgroup within the group. For example, in the case of the publishing company, suppose C and D form a subgroup because they are both old-timers, with more than twenty years of service. The committee will operate effectively only as long as its objectives and those of the subgroup coincide. However, if a decision comes along which involves the special interests of the subgroup, C and D will have conflicting loyalties. If they decide in favor of the subgroup, it means that the executive committee has ceased to be effective as a group—both C and D rate their attraction to the subgroup higher than their attraction to the committee. Hence, no great pressure can be put upon them to modify their views. True, A and B may be trying hard to persuade C and D, but without real pressure behind them since A, B, C and D are no longer functioning as a single group—the executive committee. Instead A and B have closed ranks as members of one subgroup (the non-old-timers) while C and D have closed ranks as members of another subgroup (the old-timers). If either A or B has been even slightly sympathetic to the viewpoint of the other group, as a result of the clash of interests, that sympathy is canceled. Both groups move further and further apart. In each subgroup, each member is under pressure to conform to his own subgroup.

More complicated clashes can result where the group harbors several subgroups, with several members belonging to more than one subgroup. Members may resolve their loyalties differently in different situations, thus producing constantly changing group relationships.

For example, suppose our executive committee consists of eight members. Two of them belong to a subgroup of old-timers. Two others belong to a subgroup of X University alumnae. One of the old-timers and one of the alumnae also belong to a third subgroup of ex-football heroes. In one decision facing the committee, the various special interests may be entirely unaffected, or loyalties may be resolved in favor of the committee. Then the group rules would work in favor of the committee, with extremists pressured to reach agreement with the rest of the group. However, suppose the special interests of some of the subgroups are involved in the decision. Then each member will have to resolve his loyalties in favor of the committee or subgroup—and each member may choose differently in each such decision.

Eliminating Conflicting Loyalties

If the management team is to operate effectively, it must be a highly cohesive group which commands the first loyalty of its members. It is unimportant how many subgroups may exist among its members, provided there is no conflict or rivalry between the subgroups and the group.

The way to build a strongly cohesive management team is not to try to eliminate subgroups. Rather, it is to increase the loyalty of members to the management team. It is to make the satisfactions and rewards for being part of the management team so attractive that "belonging" will be essential to its members. Thus their loyalty to the team will far outweigh their loyalty to any subgroup.

To take our executive committee again, for example, if each member finds deep satisfaction in participating in the management team, his active support and coöperation will go to the team, not to any subgroup which might imperil his continuance on the team. Top management must provide these satisfactions as the price for an effective management team.

Settling Team Conflicts

If every member of the management team finds deep rewards and satisfactions in belonging to the team, will that eliminate conflicts between team members? Of course not. In fact, it may make the conflicts even more fiery. Since each team member is passionately concerned with achieving success for the team, he will be passionately anxious for the team to adopt what he thinks is the proper action. Disputes between members will thus tend to be more vigorously argued. There's nothing harmful about that—*provided the disputes are constructively settled.*

It is at this point, however, that team loyalty becomes impaired in many companies. When disputes arise, they are settled by the test of strength—the viewpoint which can muster the larger number of proponents wins out. Or, disputes are settled by compromise —both sides give in a little and adopt a middle ground. The difficulty with both of these solutions is that dissatisfactions remain, sometimes even festering resentments. The disputes become harmful to team loyalty because they were settled destructively.

The constructive way to settle a dispute is not by either domination or compromise—it is by integration. In the first two methods, the parties are considering only their points of difference and are attempting to harmonize them. In integration, the parties consider first their common interests, and then their points of difference. In other words, they first attempt to place the dispute in context so as to reduce it to its proper perspective. Then they reëxamine the dispute in that light to see what the real issue is—to agree on just what is the nature of the dispute. Frequently the very process of making a careful, unexcited analysis destroys the conflict.

For example, suppose our executive committee is considering publication of a manuscript, with A completely in favor, B completely opposed, C and D in the middle. If the dispute is settled purely on the basis of harmonizing conflicting viewpoints, A and B will be compelled, by a combination of domination and compromise, to accept a decision neither wants. Regardless of how conscientious A and B are, neither can work as whole-heartedly to make the decision successful as he would if his own point of view had triumphed. But suppose a different method of settling the dispute had been tried. Suppose when the different viewpoints had been expressed, the committee figuratively sat back and meditated. Why was A so strongly in favor of publication? Why was B so strongly opposed? What was their common interest, and that of C and D?

Obviously, all the editors have the common interest of successful operation of the business. The decision on whether to publish the manuscript belongs in the context of whether the publication would increase or decrease profits. Actually, A feels that the company's Winter List needs strengthening in certain areas and since the manuscript falls into one of these areas, he is in favor of its publication. What A is actually disputing about, therefore, is not the merit of the manuscript, but the need to bolster the Winter List by addition of some more titles. That is the real issue. What has happened, therefore, is that analysis of the disagreement has disclosed that the question of whether or not the manuscript should be published turns not on the merits or shortcomings of the manuscript, but on the issue of whether any more manuscripts should be published and added to the Winter List. Once the real issue has been established, the editors can proceed to a constructive settlement of the actual dispute. Whatever decision is reached on publication of this manuscript becomes almost immaterial because the real problem concerns policy on the Winter List, not individual manuscripts.

Successful and constructive settlement of team disputes requires two steps, therefore: (1) concentration on the common interests of the team so as to place the conflict in proper perspective, and (2) careful and methodical analysis of the conflict until there is a clear statement to which both groups can agree on the essential issues involved.

Group assumptions must be aired and made known before group conclusions are arrived at. This, by itself, tends to lessen tension and avoid the heated arguments which arise after conclusions are reached on the basis of different assumptions.

Morale

The good management team consists of the ingredients of people (machinery), acknowledged company and individual goals (motivation), and morale (good communication).

Good morale finds a high degree of coherence within management in expectations, arrangements for a reasonable division of activities and an acknowledged system of rewards, sanctions, communication and decision-making.

With coöperative mutual understanding, there results a collaborative management where activity is applied to the stated expectations, aided by contributions from individual members which could not be successfully ordered; new ideas are freely given; relationships develop a personal warmth; formalities exist in a generally "taken for granted" manner giving the atmosphere of extreme informality. Here communication means not only that which is formally required, but additional background which is sketched in over coffee breaks or in talking "shop" outside working hours.

Any interruption of this optimum status, any interference with continued good morale is detrimental to attainment of individual potential and will seriously hamper the effectiveness of the management team.

Any alteration from team play must be ferreted out and, like any progressive degenerative disease, must be diagnosed. This implies decisive search for the particular focus of trouble and working on that directly, as against generalized, vague, ineffective appeals for "loyalty" or "team play" or the like.

Chapter IX

Bringing Up the Reserves

The acid test of how well a company is helping its people to grow and develop into executives is the quality of its executive reserve—the pool from which promising men are drawn to fill vacant management posts. The reserve should contain an adequate number of well-coached candidates in the proper age distribution, ready to fill any present vacancy or to occupy positions not yet created but necessary as the company expands.

If there is no such reserve, it means that the experience and skills accumulated by the company's older executives are not being passed on to its younger men. Thus, a valuable asset of the business —its managerial know-how—is permitted to atrophy.

A good executive reserve requires:

1. Tapping all the available sources from which executives may come so as to get the best possible collection of candidates.

2. Selecting good prospects for future executives.

3. Developing their leadership potential to the fullest possible extent.

Up from the Ranks

Many companies take considerable pride in the number of their executives who have risen from office boy to top-level jobs. Such successes come harder these days, however. Men who started in the receiving room or other rank-and-file job within the past ten or fifteen years find that they can advance only into the first or second levels of management jobs. After that point, they are considered by their company to have hit their ceiling. There are several good reasons:

1. *Age.* Because of union seniority rules which require men to progress through each job classification, it is largely impossible for outstanding men to rise through the ranks without leaving their youth behind. By the time they get on the first rungs of the management ladder, they are considered too old to begin acquiring the experience needed for executive positions.

2. *Narrow background.* It is virtually impossible for a rank-and-file employee to move horizontally across departmental lines. Therefore, he arrives at the door to the management group with excellent knowledge and grasp of the operations of one, perhaps two, departments. The rest he'll have to learn. Even if his age doesn't disqualify him, his limited scope puts him at a distinct disadvantage competitively.

3. *Education.* It is relatively rare for men who started in the ranks to acquire a college degree. Night school courses are hard to mix with marriage, growing families and increasing expenses. But the possession of a college degree is considered in many companies virtually a "must" for holders of middle or top-level management jobs.

More and more, even where the company makes conscious and continuous efforts to keep the door open for advancement of executives from the hourly work force, it is finding this source of good men drying up. Management need not merely lament the situation and allow these factors to interfere with development of possible management potential, however. There are at least two alternatives:

1. The company can try to work out some arrangement with the union to permit one or two men in each department who show supervisory potential to move across departmental lines to any job they can fill, for the purpose of diversifying their background for possible advancement. (The company may have to compete with the union for the candidate! Unions are also alert for promising men to train for top union spots.) The company may have to agree to pay the man's current wage rate although the job to which he is transferred may pay less. It may also have to agree to special provisions on seniority rights of such men—just in case they don't advance as expected. In return, however, the union may allow such men to advance on an accelerated schedule, abrogating the seniority requirements in their cases.

Incidentally, where there are no union complications, the company could set up similar provisions merely by establishing a company policy.

2. The company may offer to pay some part or all of the tuition costs for men who are attending night college courses, or who want to attend but need financial assistance. Some companies already do this for courses directly related to the employee's current work—by refunding to the worker half, or all, the tuition cost on his satisfactory completion of the course.

Is a College Degree Necessary?

A great many companies look for their executive trainees in the college senior classes. Their greatest demand is for men with technical background (engineering, chemistry, physics), and for the past several years, the companies have not been able to recruit enough such seniors to fill their quotas. One reason is that there were not enough graduates to fill all the jobs offered. (The low birth rate of the thirties was responsible for the small classes.) Another reason is that many companies accept only the top men in their classes. Companies show less interest in the liberal arts graduate, often recruiting him as a last resort.

In a recent survey, 500 companies were asked to compare their 1956 requirements for college-level men with 1955. Their replies showed that their quotas for engineering, chemistry and physics graduates were up 28.8% in 1956 over 1955, the quotas for liberal arts graduates, on the other hand, were up only 12.2%. The same preference showed up in starting salaries offered college recruits: technical graduates averaged between $350.00 and $525.00 a month; nontechnical graduates averaged between $300.00 and $416.00 a month.

Obviously, management is proceeding on the assumption that technical graduates have the greatest potential for top executive responsibility. When asked to choose the 1951 recruit who currently shows the greatest promise, out of the 97 companies who replied, 48 companies picked engineering graduates, 28 chose commerce graduates, and 21 picked liberal arts graduates. However, in comparing the salary progress of this outstanding man hired five years ago, the liberal arts graduate ranked first:

	Average Starting Salary	Average Present Salary
48 engineering graduates	$274	$607
28 commerce graduates	263	666
21 liberal arts graduates	254	679

Clearly, management should reëxamine its thinking on the relative potentials of college graduates.

Management could also profitably reëxamine its thinking on the whole subject of recruitment of college graduates on the campus. Each year, the spectacle created by the recruitment teams sent to the colleges by industry becomes more ludicrous—in a wry sort of way. One level-headed engineering senior—who could take a detached attitude because his future is mortgaged to the Air Force—

expressed himself thusly, after viewing the proceedings for several days: "If these recruitment boys are representative of what happens to people who work for these outfits, me for Uncle Sam for life!"

What is management accomplishing by cutthroat competition for "its share" of the college crop?

(a)   It is paying far too much for the men it gets . . . even assuming the recruits will some day develop into good executives . . . even assuming the recruits stay with the company which first recruited them. Each year, the starting salaries offered graduates go up by $100 to $150 a month. In 1956, for example, starting salaries offered engineering graduates ranged from $350 to $525 a month. In 1955, the range was from $300 to $450. Company A hires a 1956 graduate at $400 a month, let's say. Can it pay the 1955 graduate whom it hired last year less than $400—or even $400? After all, the '55 man now has had a year of experience which should make him worth more than his just-graduated fellow employee. And what about the 1954 man? In other words, the inflated, beginning salaries paid college recruits are playing hob with compensation schedules at all levels of the organization.

(b)   It is laying a foundation for future morale problems which will be more difficult than any nightmare any top management man has had yet. What sort of an attitude can management expect to find in the men it is now recruiting under these conditions? Today's seniors see companies fighting tooth and nail to get their services. Can they be blamed if they acquire a slightly exaggerated evaluation of what their services are worth? How many companies "queer" their recruitment tactics by explaining to the graduate that these "beginning" salaries are pretty nearly "top" salaries—that increases will be few and far between once they are "on the job"— that somewhere along the line the graduate will have to put in a heck of a lot of work to justify his pay check? Does the company make any attempt to prepare the just-hired graduate for the resentment he will encounter within the organization from co-workers who didn't get the red-carpet treatment? And what about the attitude of those co-workers, not only to the new addition, but to their jobs and to the company? Also, let's not forget the poor soul who draws the recruitment assignment—who has to set up shop on these college campuses—bring back "alive" the quota of graduates his company wants. A more frustrating, soul-searing experience for a conscientious executive can hardly be conjured.

(c)   In its haste to acquire easily assimilable graduates, management has concentrated on, and in fact continues to stress, only the purely practical—the immediately usable—and indirectly influences faculty and curriculum of colleges and engineering schools. The result: chaotic and empty search, now, for the graduate interested in and equipped for research on the theoretical rather than the applied plane.

(d)   Acquisition practices of industry have taken on hues which plainly skirt the unethical. Consider, for example, the operation of the diary system. Here's how it works. Company XX determines to set up a new operation in 1960. It will need a given number of executive-level people. The company sends its recruitment teams to visit the college campus in the now usual manner, interviewing the 1956 graduates for background and interests, estimating their executive potential. But, the team *does not offer* employment with Company XX to any of the men interviewed. Instead, it carefully culls out the most promising of the lot, and sets up a file on each man. His name also goes on the diary. The graduates of course have gone to the best available jobs in other companies. But Company XX keeps tabs on them. As their names come up in the diary (about once a year), its personnel manager calls each man, chats with him pleasantly about his job, his progress, his future plans. Still no job offer. The recruitment team goes out again in '57, '58 and '59—and more men are added to the files and the diary, rather than the payroll. The men in whom Company XX is interested have now had several years of training and experience in their jobs. They are demonstrating in a practical way their capacities, their stability. Some may have fallen by the wayside—these names Company XX simply removes from its files (the "mistakes" did not cost Company XX one cold penny). Along about 1959, Company XX writes a letter to each man in whom it is still interested, asking him to come in for an interview. At this point, finally, Company XX comes up with a job offer—and what a job offer! It is so advantageous that the man simply can't refuse it.

Company XX has thus permitted its competitors to pay for the original orientation and training of the raw industrial recruit, bear the financial burden of selection misfits. Now that the man has proved on the job that he has executive abilities, Company XX takes over and painlessly acquires proven executive potential.

A highly successful, prominent grocery company recently made a survey of its vast top-management team. Only one of its large number of top executives is a college graduate. Promotion upward was occasioned from the ranks of store managers. Following its survey, this company engaged a consultant to "iron out the problem"—what "problem"? The success and continuing forward stride of the company make it most difficult to even define the "problem." If promotion from the ranks is to continue, must recruitment of store managers henceforth be confined to college graduates?

Aptitude and ability, spirit and zest—not an educational degree —have proven of value. Fellowship in the occupation has made for a democratic feeling that underlies the true basis for the excellent employee relations this company enjoys. It is to be hoped that the consultant selected will, by study of these factors, leave well enough alone and that he will, thereafter, transmit his findings to other segments of industry in order that they, too, will be blessed by such a "problem."

How essential is a college degree to success as an executive? More and more companies are insisting on this qualification. Yet, the records indicate that the college degree, in itself, does not necessarily contribute to the rate at which people move ahead in an organization. Analysis of the careers of hundreds of successful executives shows that those with college backgrounds and those without it have made almost identical progress. Where the company operates in a nontechnical field, the college requirement is even more unimportant. For example, a survey made at one such company showed that only 20% of its department managers are college graduates; 32% had some college; 48% had none at all. Men with college degrees took an average of 8.2 years to reach department management; men with some college required an average of 7.7 years; men with no college required an average of 8.1 years. Analyzing these results, top management concluded that the chief requirement for executive competency in its company is the possession of social skills—those temperamental and personality characteristics which enable an individual to work effectively with other people. These characteristics may or may not be increased by attendance at college.

Is this true also for top-level executive jobs? In most companies, college men predominate at the higher executive levels. Because men in top jobs must have a broad grasp of business conditions, economic trends, implications of government policies and of developments in related fields, the training and experience provided by higher education is a definite asset. But even at these levels, the man's social skills are very important—and the lack of a *formal* higher education is no real barrier to the executive competency of the alert and intelligent individual.

The power of the habit of *doing* what works best to the best result can only be attained by *doing*. Emphasis upon experience and results began with the 16th century when knowledge was divorced from use and observation. Yet in 1956 large segments of industry retain personnel managers with no cognizance of the work activity required for efficient operation *in the company*—hire these screeners of future potential on the strength of the transmission of a certain body of general settled knowledge evidenced by a college degree albeit in business administration! The myth (part of that greater myth of Executive Development Programs) that our schools are an open sesame to the Utopia of the desired executive "crop," precisely tailored and numbered to fill the need, has cost industry much valuable time and money—that could well have been utilized to great advantage in our increasingly competitive economy.

How can any company truly prosper or continue to prosper when its greatest potential lies unused, discouraged, and, often, unknown?

In short, a college degree indicates a certain amount of exposure to broadening influences helpful in executive positions—*it doesn't guarantee success* in such positions. Making such a requirement, therefore, without reference to the individual involved, means that a company is unnecessarily limiting its sources of potential executives.

Pirating

Hiring executives from other companies is a more or less popular way to fill the executive reserve—depending on whether you're hiring or losing the executive. It is hard to estimate how widespread the practice is, because the cries of pain more often relate to the quality rather than to the quantity of the men involved. Where a man is recruited directly to fill an executive vacancy, he provides a clear example of pirating—even though his company may say, "We will not stand in your way." But it is not uncommon for companies to bring men into their organizations who are marked for executive appointments after serving a relatively short period. These are the examples of hidden piracy which cloud the statistics on the extent of the practice.

For example, in a recent survey, 62 company presidents were asked for their opinion on how executive vacancies were filled in most companies today. They replied:

Method	Vacancies Filled	Times Mentioned
Pirating (men are hired from other companies)	10%	45
Automatic (able men come naturally to the top)	15	41
Consultants (candidates are studied and recommended by outside consultants)	10	35
Compromise (least unlikely candidate is appointed)	5	24
Merit (men are promoted from within the company on the basis of demonstrated ability and favorable work record)	55	50
Miscellaneous (nepotism, seniority, politics, etc.)	5	31

The presidents were then asked to tell how the last three executive vacancies had been filled in their own companies:

40 companies	Last three vacancies filled from within the company.
12 companies	Two of the last three vacancies filled from within the company.
8 companies	Two of last three vacancies filled from outside the company.
2 companies	Last three vacancies filled from outside the company.

On the basis of these replies, it would appear that roughly 18% of executive appointments are made from *outside* the company. But the figure would be much higher if the cases of "hidden" piracy could be estimated.

Hiring "ready-made" executives permits a company to fill an executive job immediately, or within a comparatively short period. Also, the man's success in his previous management posts provides a measure of his probable success in the new position. However, there are several serious disadvantages:

1. *"Mistakes" are very costly.* Even though the man may have proved successful in his previous position, transplanting may not

work. There may have been special factors at work in his previous setup which contributed to his success. Their absence in his new environment will make him less effective. Or, he may be unable to win the coöperation of the management group. His "new broom" ideas may be impractical in the new organization, leaving him with a sense of misfit or frustration. Scores of *reasons* may be enumerated, but whatever the reason, if he doesn't come up to expectations, the losses to the company, both tangible and intangible, will be considerable.

2. *Ready-made executives need retailoring.* Unless the man's experience includes some in the company's field of operations, he may need a considerable amount of tutoring and orientation until he gets his feet under him in the new position. This is particularly true in management jobs where familiarity with the company products or customers is a vital part of the responsibility of the post. The importance of having previous industry experience decreases in the top-level management jobs, but some specific or comparable experience is essential for planning and policy making.

3. *Ready-made executives come high.* Salary considerations alone will not always attract the man the company wants for a particular job. Especially in the upper-middle and top executive echelons, the man may already be earning all the salary he wants. He may even be willing to take less salary in making a move, provided he gets an opportunity in the new position for a freer hand in day-to-day operations, or a chance at some ownership of the business. If the company agrees, it may have to make similar concessions to its other executives to keep them happy.

4. *They disturb morale.* Unless new men are brought in at the lower levels of management, they inevitably face serious problems of acceptance, both by their colleagues and by men at lower levels. Although there may be no person in the company really qualified for promotion, there is deep resentment about the importation of an outsider to fill the position.

The experience of one company which recently faced this situation demonstrates the extent to which this resentment can carry. When a position in middle management unexpectedly became vacant, the company found it had two men to consider for promotion to the post. After looking into their experience and ability, it became obvious that neither one was a good bet for promotion at that time. However, the company decided to give one of the men a chance at the job, rather than recruiting someone from outside the company. After several months, the man's incompetence could no longer be overlooked, and the company was forced to dismiss him as it was not possible to return him to his old job and no other position was available. It then promoted the second man to the job, found its misgivings again confirmed. At that point, it went outside and selected an executive with an excellent record, who seemed well suited to the job. However, the circumstances preceding his appointment had so impaired the morale of the executive group that he was never able to establish the working relationships essential to proper performance of his job. He finally "resigned." The company was by now pretty well stymied. After more consideration and more delay, it finally resorted to the temporary expedient of splitting up the job among several of the executives. Meanwhile still a fourth man, from inside the company, was groomed to take over. The entire process took well over three years. The final appointee is still learning his job. This could have been done with the first man. The company still refuses to estimate the cost of the incident in actual financial outlay as well as in reduced efficiency and irretrievable damage to morale.

Even where resentments don't reach such proportions, going outside the company to fill important management posts is poor policy. Able men in lower-echelon jobs inevitably begin to question their future prospects for advancement. Many will seize their first opportunity to move on to other firms, thus making orderly development of executive talent within the company even more difficult.

If it is imperative to fill a management post from outside the company, the decision and the reasons for making it should be explained to all members of the management group. In addition, any men who might be expected to feel cheated of possible promotion should be told in private interviews of the reasons they were passed over in this case. All of this communication should take place *before* the company starts looking around for possible candidates. Most important of all, the management group must be convinced that top management recognizes its obligation to provide opportunities for its executives—as proved by the specific action which will be taken to avoid repetition of the incident in the future. Unless top management adopts this attitude sincerely, it can set up policy, issue directives and hold executive development conferences until the cows come home—executive development in the company will remain a farce and a fable.

If Not Pirating, What?

There are at least two alternatives to pirating where a company needs to fill an executive post immediately:

1. *Hiring part-time executives.* The company may find it practical to secure the services of a competent executive who is already holding down a job in another company. Such an executive can act as a part-time employee as long as the company needs his services, while acting as a consultant in training the man being groomed for the job.

If this procedure is practical in the company's circumstances, it obviates the problem of having to take immediate action in filling an executive post although the person in line for the job is not yet ready to assume it. The outside executive is patently a stopgap only, and thus avoids the morale difficulties he would encounter as a permanent member of the staff. His services give the company a breathing space in which to build up the knowledge and experience needed by the man scheduled for the job so as to insure his success after promotion.

Some companies are beginning to draw on the accumulated knowledge and skills of *retired* executives to supplement the management know-how of their management team. Typically, such executives have retired from important posts in large companies and are eager to keep a hand in on management, particularly in the smaller companies. Some of these retired executives work part-time as regular members of the staff, others act as consultants. They can be especially invaluable to the smaller company because of the breadth of business experience and skill which they can bring to its limited management.

2. *Hiring management consultants.* A company which must fill an executive post immediately but finds its scheduled replacement lacking in the requisite skills, may promote the man anyway —and then use a professional management consultant to supplement his management know-how. Consultants help not only at the operational level, but also at the policy level, either by suggesting suitable policy decisions or by increasing the skills of management people so that better policy decisions will be made in the future. In the case of the inadequately qualified replacement, for example, the consultant's services may range from advice in situations where the man is inadequately informed to suggestions on how the executive can increase his effectiveness by reading, college courses, etc.

Small companies tend to shy away from this method of supplementing management skills because of the belief that such services are feasible for only the large companies. To the contrary, however, management consultants are particularly effective in counseling small businessmen on matters requiring knowledge or experience which would not normally be acquired in small-company operations. For example, an outside consultant was called in by one company after refusal of a bank loan left it in a precarious financial situation. The consultant found that the emergency had arisen because the manager had made some large cash purchases of raw materials. The buys were excellent, but when the company's anticipated cash flow from sales fell below his expectations, the business was faced with a shortage of working capital. The consultant was able to suggest a source from which the needed loan was secured. He also worked with the manager to develop a procedure for avoiding a similar predicament in the future. He suggested adoption of a cash budget. The manager was not familiar with this technique but was willing to try the advice. Together with the consultant, he worked up figures representing expected sales for the next year. This projected figure provided him with a base on which to estimate the company's incoming cash, plan his purchases accordingly. After the budget was in use for several months, the manager discovered that the company's receipts and disbursements followed a recognizable pattern. After further testing and revision of his budget, he was able to take advantage of "bargains" within the framework of his budget with confidence that he would not strip the company of its working capital.

Costs involved in the use of a management consultant vary widely, depending largely on how much time he is required to devote to the company's affairs. A company can only decide on the feasibility of such assistance by contacting some of the management consultant firms in its area and discussing its situation with them.

Completely overlooked by many firms are other sources of technical and practical knowledge, available at nominal cost usually. The firm's bank, for example. Its manager or representative is a veritable gold mine of up-to-date information on industry trends, community factors affecting business, etc. The banks are displaying increasing awareness of their potentially invaluable role in aiding industry. In the Far West, Midwest and East, for example, the banks, by their recent mergers, are attempting to provide better service—and in many cases unique service—to managements whose needs can be filled by consultation with bank specialists. As against the fear that such mergers would detract from banker-industry relationships, many instances have been found in recent months of an increase in the willingness and ability of the banks to aid the industries in the areas they serve by anticipating, as well as filling, industry needs. And because of their mergers, the banks are now in a position to provide a staff of bank officers who have intimate, firsthand knowledge of the industries the banks wish to serve.

Another overlooked, valuable specialist is the accountant. His services are used in keeping books in shape, preparing necessary reports, etc. Rarely, however, does the company call on his services when making policy decisions on inventory, price adjustments which may change its tax situation, purchase or sale of business assets which may have tax implications, etc. He is only asked to handle the effects of policy decisions after they are made—when in fact he could have contributed valuable information which might even have affected the decision made. The same is true of services of other specialists. The company will insist that its lawyer check over a union contract before it signs, for instance. It rarely asks him to sit in on negotiation sessions with the union—where his advice and experience may be extremely useful in resolving disputes or effecting compromises.

Selecting Executive Timbre

Hiring men for management positions is largely catch-as-catch-can in most business enterprises. Candidates are assembled on someone's recommendation, either inside or outside the company; or through employment agencies or consultants; or by help-wanted advertising. The candidate is interviewed by two or three management people who look into his past record, "pass him around" to try to appraise his executive potential. The man who makes the best impression gets the position. Decisions are based on intuitive judgment—flying "by the seat of the pants" technique—in most cases, amounting to a personality preference formed during the interview with the candidate.

For example, three junior executives were hired in one company last year. In each case, the candidates were found by the vice-president by securing recommendations from his personal friends. (Most of the candidates were not personally known to the men who *recommended* them.) The men filled out the usual application forms and submitted their resume sheets, after which interviews were scheduled for them with the vice-president, at half-hour intervals. At the interview, the executive had the candidates go over their qualifications (although they were already on record), and then let the conversation take "its natural course." In the case of one of the jobs, for example, he started off by commenting on the morning paper's headline. The first applicant made a neutral rejoinder, which displeased the executive. He asked a few more perfunctory questions and closed the interview. The second applicant expressed an opinion at variance with the executive's view, stuck to his guns in the ensuing discussion. The third applicant also expressed a contrary opinion, but perceived his error and backtracked well enough to recover lost ground. He emerged with the job because the executive's judgment on the interviews was: the first applicant was too wishy-washy; the second was stubborn and stupid; the third was willing to see the other side of a question, not too proud to admit error, willing to learn from his superiors.

Actually, the executive's judgment might be right—despite the apparent capriciousness of the evidence supporting the reasons he gave. In years of experience in working with and judging men, his ability to make correct "guesses" might have become well developed. For the majority, however, intuition is very much hit-or-miss. Most men in management posts welcome any objective help they can get in assessing the potentials of men as executives.

How Good Are Interviews?

Many studies are being made in an attempt to discover methods of testing men on their leadership potential. To date, however, chief reliance is still being placed on judgments formed in the course of personal interviews with the candidate. Although time consuming and trying, the interview system is used because there is, as yet, no other workable system to use.

Interviewing can be made more scientific, however; less dependent on instinct or mood:

1. *Advance screening.* Since interviews are costly in terms of the time and energy of busy executives, candidates who don't meet the preliminary standards should be culled out as early as possible. Most companies require preliminarily: (a) specified minimum education or experience, (b) age within given brackets, and (c) no serious blots against the man anywhere in his past record. If a review of his resume or experience record shows that he apparently qualifies, he's passed on to the second barrier.

Be careful that this advance screening doesn't cull out not only the unsuitable candidates—but also men who would do an excellent job despite their lack of some of the mandatory qualifications. If the preliminary standards are placed at some arbitrary point which is not really significant in terms of the job to be filled, you may be eliminating good management material without even preliminary consideration. Take for example, the age bracket. Very often desirable age standards are set for men entering various management levels. But these limits should be understood to be *desirable* only—not mandatory. A man who is three or four years over the top age limit may have "lost" those years in advanced study, or in working for the money with which to continue his education, or in job experimentation to discover his proper niche. In other words, the very discrepancy which apparently eliminates him from consideration may be the tip-off to his ambition, drive, perseverance, forethought: the very factors you would rate highly in selecting him for your executive reserve. Yet you would never get to see him at all, since he would have been rejected on the first review of his record as too old.

Incidentally, the age standard as applied to a candidate for an executive position highlights a major problem in many companies. Pension plans in industry—hailed as a major incentive in holding on to valuable executive talent—are also hamstringing industry in filling executive posts. The age limitations in pension plans have been incorporated into the fabric of industry's employment techniques to such an extent that it has become highly questionable whether pension plans are a blessing or a curse as applied to executive-level jobs. In company after company, an executive in the 45–50 age bracket—when he is best qualified by mature experience to really pull his weight—cannot be hired without upsetting the company's entire pension plan setup. These are young men in every sense of the word as applied to executive jobs—industry needs them sadly. Yet such are the barriers that in New York City (as well as in many other metropolitan areas) special organizations have been set up to serve as placement experts for "forty plus" executives. This in a period when large segments of industry are bemoaning the "shortage" of executives with mature judgment and experience! It is encouraging to note that the combined talents of the banking and insurance industries are now being devoted, albeit somewhat belatedly, to finding methods of easing this dilemma in which industry finds itself.

2. *Preliminary testing.* Candidates who survive the first screening are then tested. All companies routinely administer a series of tests to executive candidates. Typically, these may consist of the American Council of Education *Psychological Examination* (mental abilities); the Guilford-Martin *Inventory of Factors STDCR, Inventory of Factors GAMIN,* and *Personnel Inventory I* (temperament); the Allport-Vernon *Study of Values* (motivation); and the Kuder *Preference Record,* Form BB (interests).

These and other similar tests are standard and can be bought on the open market. But of course they are only as good as the clinical insight of those who interpret them. They cannot substitute for good judgment—they merely aid in formulating judgment. In most companies, men are not eliminated on the basis of the test results but the results are communicated to the interviewer, to aid him by suggesting possible areas of weakness or strength in the individual which might not be otherwise discovered in the interview.

3. *Personality probing.* Those candidates who survive both the advance screening and the testing are then interviewed. The planned interview can produce a fairly good picture of the candidate's personality, provided the interviewer knows what to look for —and how. He can test for emotional control by staging a dis-

cussion where the applicant must meet arguments. Does he meet them forthrightly? or does he vacillate, become agitated? If the interviewer suddenly confronts him with a sharp disagreement, does he falter, backtrack, try to reword his statement in accordance with the interviewer's apparent opinion? Does he withstand the attack with poise? When asked about his life goals, is he coherent, specific? Is he a good listener—or is what you are saying going in one ear and out the other while he waits for a pause to go on with what *he* was saying? Looking at the total individual, can you see him as an executive some day?

The ability of an interviewer to reach sound decisions on the management potential of the men he interviews is not easily acquired. There is no magic formula on which he can rely to separate the leaders from the duds. He learns early in the game that it is not enough to "bet on brains." An executive must be intelligent; but also he must have competitive drive, social skills, better than average emotional controls and defenses to withstand the strain and pressure of an executive's job. And above all, he must be able to get along with other people at all levels. None of these qualifications are tangible, measurable or testable. But as he continues to gain experience in observing men *and checking his conclusions against actual results,* the interviewer will begin to acquire a sixth sense—an educated instinct—by means of which he can recognize a potential executive, no matter what face or personality he happens to wear.

The extent to which management people are aware of their fallibility in executive selection is well illustrated by a recent analysis of how 200 executive appointments were made in 62 companies. Only 33 were decided by the president acting alone, or by the president and one other company official. Usually three or four persons participated in the selection of the new executive. Eight or ten persons were consulted in many cases. And in one case, no fewer than twenty different people participated in the selection! (No report on the soundness of *that* decision, nor how long it took to arrive at the decision.)

Psychological Testing

Most companies routinely require candidates for executive positions to complete a battery of psychological tests. Yet, to date, no test or group of tests has been found which can be used by every company to determine the executive potential of an individual. There are some 600 to 700 standard tests in existence—testing intelligence, proficiency, aptitude, vocational interests, personality. Yet it is entirely possible that none of these tests would be of any help to a particular company. This has been amply proved by the experience of companies who bought "test packages," quickly found they had wasted time, money and effort—not to mention the embarrassment of situations created in some instances of psychological "rejects."

Psychological tests can be made effective for a company but only in this way:

1. Developing the tests specifically for that company, after careful study of its organization, policy and people.

2. Having the test results interpreted by skilled experts.

3. Requiring constant evaluation and correlation of the test results with actual company experience.

In one manufacturing company, for example, a team of psychologists spent three months investigating daily operations, the requirements of the executive posts, the kind of men who had succeeded in management jobs. They then constructed a trial "battery" of tests which was administered to a control group. After evaluation of the test results, the battery was revised, tested again, revised, etc., for another three months. The final version was then adopted and used in the company for two years. At the end of that period, the team returned, reëvaluated the battery on the basis of company experience during those two years. It has been constantly emphasized to the management group that the purpose of constructing the battery is to find a *tool to aid* them in selection of executive talent—not to find a tool to do the selection.

In short, psychological tests must be tailor-made for the company by experts and interpreted by experts. But the experts can help management by using down-to-earth language, free of professional jargon. The psychologist in these tailor-made situations must be made to face the fact that if his services are to be effective, he must be understood, wholly and not in part, by the industrial, engineering, or sales executive who will actually be using the testing procedures to evaluate candidates. Psychological testing is still on the proving ground and many sincere and devoted experts in this field, by failing to give thought to clarity and simplification, have made their paths, and the future of their profession in the business and industrial sphere, neither effective nor attractive. The use of in-the-profession terminology is impractical and disturbing to an executive who cannot take time out for a course in psychology or practical psychiatry.

More and more companies are turning to the services of professionals to do the psychological testing for them. These outside professionals test applicants for executive positions by giving them a combination of tests and intensive depth interviews. When these are completed, the professional draws up a report for the company, evaluating the results of the tests and interviews in terms of what they reveal of the applicant's personality. However, except in rare cases where serious psychological disturbances are disclosed, the report does not make a recommendation to the client company on whether or not the applicant should be hired. The report is intended, again, as only additional information for the company to consider in coming to its decision.

The results of the tests can suggest areas of weakness or strength in the individual tested. With these clues in mind, the interviewer can probe for evidence to prove or disprove the test findings. However, the test findings cannot be used as the sole criterion for deciding whether an individual is a good prospect as an executive. There are too many variables in the work situation, too little knowledge of group dynamics, far too much pontificating about and far too little investigation of the elements of success in executive positions. The tests, if properly constructed for the company's needs, can assist management in arriving at a judgment. But until there is much more research and evaluation of testing procedures, business must continue to rely on interviewing, and the impressions formed in those contacts, in choosing men for executive positions.

Will He Be an Executive Some Day?

Executive ability is not a tangible, definable skill. It can't be measured by a work sample since it depends on constantly changing combinations of skills and characteristics. But in practice, a measure *is* needed. An answer must be given when you look at an individual and wonder whether he will do well in an executive position.

One factor to consider is the man's areas of satisfaction. Mere ability to do something is not the important factor in executive success. Rather, the important factor is the man's motivation, his life goal. Does he feel that making money is important? Then he'll put his heart into a job where profit is the main objective—and money will compensate him for doing all day a thing he doesn't particularly like. But take the same situation and put into it a man who doesn't think making money is important. Will he—*can* he—do well on that job over the long haul?

Consider his emotional control. Executive jobs put a heavy strain on a man's emotions and defenses. More than one man has broken under the torment of bucking the pressure from above and the inertia from below. Is this man sensitive, brittle? Will he have the toughness frequently required of a good executive? And the compassion?

Try to evaluate his sense of humor. A good executive uses it more often than the telephone. More than any other trait, it is standard equipment for good executives—men whose job it is to get things done through other people. As you look at your candidate, try to imagine how he'll react when the third man comes into his office on the same miserable morning with bad news. Or when the report he's worked on long and hard, and presented proudly to his superior, is dismissed with a single glance, "Oh, we've decided to shelve that project. Now, instead. . . ."

Try to place him in a staff conference two years from now, five years from now. How will he get along with irascible George, domineering Frank, shy but brilliant Walter? Will they like him? Do you feel that he'll wear well?

Is he the type who generates interest? An executive must be interested before he can interest others. His ambivalence toward any company objective will be reflected throughout the ranks of his subordinates despite his failure to openly oppose the project or objective.

Is he the type who will help people unlearn the wrong meanings? Will he lead in taking the positive approach by handling situations sensibly which, when handled otherwise, may become intolerably stressful? Has he, or can he be developed to have, the ability of structuralizing or maintaining a management communications network in such a way that origin and destination of messages become known; that instructions for action are simple and clear; and that, in case of doubt, messages can be checked upon?

Has he the flexibility for alteration and change as the need arises? Can he detect too rigid controls, and on spotting them, devise means of avoiding the red tape that results from such controls?

Has he a reasonable level of physical capacity? Can he evaluate information he cannot get by himself? Will he make decisions on the basis of, rather than in spite of, facts and policies?

Is he the type, who will become a marionette, mentally plaster-casted by routine, and, who, because of this, will have no time for new ideas and die of alleged economic attrition?

Has he a maddening insistence on logical definition of terms without knowledge or sense of the true worth of the whole subject?

Has he a feel for the objective present—and for the subjective future? Does he have insight into the requirements of now, today? Will he be appreciative of what is ripe for development?

Can he write or orally explain problems in terms so lucid that the complexity of their solution is not made more involved?

Is he the individual who will make for effective coördination of your executive floor: helping each person make his coöperative contribution to success by *doing his particular share* of the whole duty?

If you can find out: has his wife narrowed him to the anxious acquisitiveness of the prodded husband?

Can he take discipline, and by doing so, spread informative techniques to those about him?

Is he the type against whose passion for power, reason and morality are helpless?

Does he, by his answers, suggest an *insistence* on being let alone, or, conversely, does he dislike solitude and live in perpetual dependence on what is outside himself?

Beware: those who show the ravages of fear and care—the shrill voice and hasty steps, those with the too complacent look, those who feel malice, are fond of talking and vehemence, are quick to blame others and praise themselves.

Does he have any mannerisms which annoy you? or which would annoy others on the executive staff? Are they important enough— or so trivial—that they would strain relationships? The nonsmoking executive who passed over a chain-smoking candidate after considerable conscientious struggling was probably right. Think what ten or twenty years of having smoke continuously blown in his face would do to him.

Our Competitors Steal Them

The departure of a management person to a competitor is costly, not only in terms of development investment, but also in the disarrangement of the progression pattern which the company has erected. The company will usually insist that its executives leave for more money, or for a title, or for prestige reasons. But digging below the surface has shown that relatively few men leave for these reasons. In the majority of cases, the men leave not because of what they are being offered elsewhere but because of what they are *not* being offered in their present jobs. They leave because they have lost incentive—doubt their future with the company. Sometimes, their attitude results from being passed over for promotion, or from an equally obvious incident; in other cases, the attitude builds up from a gradual accumulation of incidents, unimportant in themselves but showing a negative pattern:

1.   The firm informs a promising man that he is in line for advancement, but as vacancies at managerial levels occur they are invariably filled from outside the company with no explanation to the man or the staff.

2.   Men are promoted to responsible jobs but find that actual authority is retained at the top and they are, in effect, glorified errand boys.

3.   Able men find themselves in dead-end positions in which they cannot acquire any real management experience. They are passed up when openings develop because they haven't *proved themselves*.

These and similar instances boil down to one fundamental failing: lack of real communication. Frequently the perpetual pressure of work carried by management people leaves them no time for informal chats, for the small gestures implying recognition of work well done. The situation is frequently aggravated because the very same executives who excuse their failure to recognize good work because of lack of time are, on the other hand, never too busy to "raise the roof" over mistakes. Where such a pattern develops and persists, subordinates inevitably become discouraged, and the best men drift away.

Many companies suffer another problem: their management levels are relatively few, and men must stay in the same job for long periods, appearing to make no progress. Such companies should stress their corresponding advantages. Their promising men don't "get lost." They have more real responsibility, more opportunity to participate directly in top-level management discussions and decisions. And this opportunity occurs far earlier than it would in companies with a more complicated management set-up. The individual contribution of executives in the company with a small management staff is clearly apparent. Since there are fewer people there is much less chance for inertia to permit inefficient or unqualified men to ride along on the efforts of others.

What executives want, as revealed in interviews and informal discussions, boils down to three essentials: status, management responsibility, and adequate compensation.

Status: In many companies there is astonishing lack of recognition of the importance, especially to beginning executives, of the symbols of executive status. Frequently, the junior executive cares very strongly for the larger desk, the extra chair, the private office, the rug on the floor, etc. Obviously, these things are unimportant in themselves—their value lies in the respect which they command from rank-and-file employees. Omission of such symbols is puzzling, makes for a feeling of uncertain status. The employees whom the executive is supervising look for an explanation for the absence of the appropriate symbols, assume that it means the executive hasn't really "made the grade." The result is an indirect challenge to prestige, a lowered respect for the man, and impaired morale in his department.

Complaints about lack of symbols of executive standing are rarely made by the executive to his superior. The matter appears so trivial that he feels hesitant about attempting to explain the effect of the situation on his own job performance. Furthermore, he really believes that his superior does understand the importance of the symbols of authority. Therefore, if the superior has not bestowed them upon the subordinate, there must be a good reason. The subordinate invariably assumes the reason to be his own unsatisfactory performance.

Management Responsibility: Executives often complain that they are in effect glorified office boys who are assigned the routine jobs, the research projects, the "digging out the facts" assignments. Actual decisions, however, are made by their superiors. They feel that part of their value to the company should be their judgment and their decision-making ability. Unless these abilities are given expression and opportunity, the executive actually is not an executive. He is not working through others to secure company goals or effectuate company plans—only his superior is doing this. If the man is continued in such a routinized job for a considerable period, he either settles down and loses his initiative, or he runs for his life.

If investigation of such a complaint discloses that more than 50% of the subordinate's work consists of research or similar activities on matters which then go to the superior for decision, you might take a fresh look at your organization chart. Is the subordinate's job really an executive position? If so, who is discharging the executive responsibilities which according to the chart belong to that job? Has the man's superior really looked at the subordinate's job as it functions in actual practice? Are present arrangements a carry-over from the old days when he had no subordinate, or when his subordinate was not an able man?

Compensation: For trainee executives, compensation is important but minor compared with the intangible rewards they look for in their jobs: opportunity to advance, opportunity to learn, opportunity to work with able men, an environment which stimulates, superiors who seem to take a personal interest in their development and advancement.

Any company which loses able men often to better opportunity elsewhere has a real problem to look into, but one which may be worth more to the company when solved than other seemingly more important problems.

Underwriting the teaching philosophy of Kant, a large segment of industry seems to assume it practical to attend most to those candidates of "middle" ability, on the assumption that able men can and will help themselves.

There are facts and forces which clearly tend to encourage an almost unconscious acceptance of mediocrity. Excellent management potential senses this and runs away. The management team must determine, therefore, whether it will concentrate on the excellent, or accept the average, with its consequent universal spread of mediocrity.

Chapter X

Depth: Executive Floor
Without Flaw

You have been doing a good deal of pondering and analyzing since you began reading this book. You've looked at your Executive Floor—studied its occupants and its operations. You recognize which of your management people are weak reeds, and why. You know which men are solid, loyal, worthy of your best efforts to provide them with a rewarding, vibrant environment.

Some of your decisions were obvious, though difficult. A few you may still be sweating out. But you've started wheels moving which you hope will eventually have your executives and your Executive Floor operating at peak effectiveness.

You still have one more objective, imperative from both your personal and business viewpoints. You want your executives to do a superlative job—and to find solid rewards and satisfactions while doing it. This is necessary from your personal viewpoint because enthusiastic men are warm, good to work with, stimulating and enriching to your own vision and outlook. It is mandatory from the business viewpoint because you must keep these zealous, talented men working for *your* company—not your competitor's.

How is it done? What is the secret of keeping able men in their jobs despite "better" offers from other companies? Why does the Executive Floor in some companies resemble a one-night stand, a steppingstone to a better job elsewhere? As one executive acidly commented: "In our company, you can't follow the game without a program to tell you who the players are—this week."

If your Executive Floor has a revolving door, it is obviously not giving your people the satisfaction they require to be happy in their jobs. In some cases, the missing ingredient may seem to be almost trivial in relation to the results of its absence: a larger office; a title; a standing invitation to the weekly lunch with the top brass. It may seem trivial, but it most certainly isn't so minor an item if it represents to the man a symbol of success, status, or "belonging." In other cases, the missing ingredient may be harder to supply. The man's needs are intangible, complex—he wants to feel that his contribution is unique; or that his position provides scope for all his talents; or that he's working for a company that is progressive, growing, sincerely interested in its people.

In most companies, satisfaction of these tangible and intangible needs of executive personnel is possible only to the extent that top management recognizes and assumes responsibility for their satisfaction.

Challenge—Let Him See It

Someone once remarked that the true executive is never happy doing a job he knows. Every top management person will agree—

wearily. As soon as your bright boy feels he's completely "on top" of his job, he's in trouble. So are you.

The talented executive needs challenge in his job. It is a deep and genuine need of his personality to be always striving upwards —to be always seeking new responsibilities, or more complex ones, or more demanding ones. He can be *very* trying.

One way, therefore, to keep your much-wanted zealous executive tied to his job (and to your company) is to recognize and fulfill this deep need of his nature.

Your bright subordinate needs challenge? Well, give him a good one—your job. Enlarge his horizons by giving him the opportunity to learn all the ramifications and nuances of your position—from its top functions down to the last piddling detail of its routine controls.

Let him start by watching you in operation. One or two days a week, relieve him of his usual responsibilities—make it his job to sit with you in your office (quietly, if possible) and watch how you handle the situations and people who require your attention. Take him along to the conferences you attend, the luncheon meetings, the briefing sessions. Let him read the memos, the reports, the letters that cross your desk; and listen to your replies.

When you feel that he has soaked up as much as he can by observation, start to do a little explaining. Let him ask questions. Then, bit by bit, ease him on to the next step—participation in your job.

Participation—Let Him Do It

The true executive will be content to observe for just so long. Pretty soon, he'll start itching to be in there pitching. When that time comes with your bright subordinate, let him begin to handle selected pieces of your job. This doesn't mean that you delegate parts of your job to him. Responsibility for the whole job continues in your hands—you merely let him do some of the work for you, according to your standards of competence and under your close supervision and control.

For example, your subordinate has been looking over your shoulder while you analyzed reports from the various departments under your supervision. He has watched you send some back for further facts, or better figures, or more study of the conclusions. He has watched you synthesize the information on the various reports with information coming to your desk from other sources, prepare your own report and recommendations. Now, let your subordinate begin participating in your job by analyzing these reports for you. Give him detailed instructions on the factors he must take into consideration, how to weigh one against another in evaluating the validity of the reports. Instruct him also on how to check the reports by correlating the information they contain with that received from other sources. Ask him to prepare rough drafts of the summary report you must send out. As he does the work, check closely on his methods and results every step of the way. Stop him whenever he makes a mistake, have him correct his error before going on to the next operation. Remember, you are not now giving him leeway for errors; the work must be done properly—it is going out as your work, over your signature.

When your subordinate has learned this aspect of your work sufficiently well to be able to step in and do it for you whenever you wish him to do so, you may proceed in the same way to teach him another aspect of your job. In each case, the job duties continue to remain your responsibility—you are merely allowing your subordinate to learn how to handle them should it be necessary or desirable for him to do so at any time.

This "sitting-in" on your job should be recognized as an aspect of your subordinate's regular responsibilities. If the time required means that he cannot handle all the duties now part of his job, some of his duties should be assigned elsewhere. Not only your subordinate, but also the rest of the group, should understand what is going on, and why.

Depth—Get Four of Him

When your subordinate has been broken in on a number of the functions of your job, you should start the process going all over again with your next-most-promising subordinate. Have him start sitting in with you—while at the same time you keep your first subordinate at steadily more difficult assignments, always with your standards of good, thorough work to live up to.

And after your second subordinate is well along the road to being able to handle parts of your job, start the process with a third subordinate, and a fourth. Each man will come along at a different pace, handle himself differently. But as time goes on, you will have developed a series of competent backstops, any one of whom can carry on in your place when necessary, eventually move up to take over your position when you go up the line.

At an appropriate point in this process, incidentally, you will have instructed each of your subordinates how they should begin to develop *their* subordinates along similar lines.

The net result, if this process is faithfully observed, will be that each executive will be enthusiastically performing his job, learning the functions of a higher job, and carefully training his subordinates in the functions of his job. There will be two or three men able to handle, although perhaps with varying skill, every important executive function. The Executive Floor will have depth as well as breadth of skill.

Feed Him Kale

Experience has taught us that business executives do not work for salary alone. It is not uncommon, in fact, to see a man go from a well-paying position in one company to a job in another company which pays less but appears to him to offer more opportunity. He's rarely thinking about money when he talks about opportunity in making such a move. If you probe a bit, you'll find him telling you that he thinks he'll have more voice in the management of the company; or more independence of action in discharging his responsibilities; or a more stimulating group of associates.

You could learn a lot about this subject by talking to the doctors and psychiatrists who number executives among their patients. They could talk for hours about the incidence of hypertension, physical illness, personality disorders among executives in direct response to the frustrating, unrewarding work they were doing. Why frustrating, unrewarding? Surely a man must have a basic interest in his work to be able to rise to executive levels? The medical men will tell you that in fact executives have a deep interest in their work, even the routine aspects. They care a great deal about doing a competent job, achieving desired results. The frustration and lack of reward arise from the repeated experience of seeing their hard work nullified by a stupid or stubborn act or omission of the top brass. They arise from watching the same nonsense go on week after week in management conferences.

To keep your executive happy in his work, all you have to do is to treat him like an executive. Feed him the right kind of work and lots of it; give him responsibility for getting it done; give him competent men to direct in doing the work; give him the glory for accomplishing the job; let him raise his voice in forming, rather than in approving, decisions; keep him believing in the value of his achievements and in the reality of his present and future goals inside the company.

In short, you keep your executive happy by *building in* his job satisfactions, so that they arise from the substance of his daily work activities—not by tacking them on, so that they in effect attempt to disguise the emptiness and barrenness of his work efforts.

Those Executive Prerogatives

It is in the companies whose top managements do not understand what makes executives "tick" that you will find the custom-crafted or designer-decorated executive offices, the platoons of vice-presidents, the executive elevator, parking space, company supplied automobile or plane or yacht, the company paid club membership, and the astronomical executive entertainment fund.

Aren't these rewards important? To a certain extent—and for certain people. Some executives find their satisfaction primarily in the status or prestige their positions secure for them in the community or within the organizational hierarchy. For such men, a title and the other executive status symbols are extremely important. The symbols are also important to the executive who feels insecure about his place. To him, they are reassuring signs; tangible proofs that he is doing all right in his job.

To the rest of your executives, a title and the other "rewards" may have as many negative as positive connotations. To begin with, the symbols are carefully graduated up the scale of executive positions —thus creating jealousies and increasing tensions—complicating the difficulties of fostering team spirit among executives. Secondly, the "rewards" usually add up to more pressure on the executive. The luncheon conference with the top brass or with important customers, for example, means that two or three hours of his day are "shot"—and the higher the executive position, the more such conferences. The satisfaction of being *on the inside* which a title may carry can be largely negated by the increased pressure on the executive to watch his public utterances. His increased status in the community means a lot of extra work too—such as participation in community fund drives, speech making, obligatory social obligations. His increased status in the company means less freedom to experiment, make mistakes—he has a position to uphold and false moves may imperil it. It also costs him friendships built up over the years with men who stay behind in the lower levels. There is tacit understanding that *more suitable* associations should be formulated by the executive.

Another point, rarely brought to light: men whose rise up through the executive ranks is based on sheer ability often feel bitterly resentful of colleagues who have reached the same elevated position primarily on the basis of a talent for *getting along* with top management.

The multiplication of titles which has taken place in many companies during recent years is another negative factor. Searching for a method of recognizing an executive's fine contribution, his company in many instances settled on giving him a title, in addition to a raise. Since the money incentive has been largely eroded by taxes, the title was considered the primary reward. Also, very importantly, the title pleased the executive's wife. (Keeping the wives of executives happy amounts to a religion in some large companies.) However, the continuing creation of titles has cheapened the value and prestige of this reward. Also, it has created some truly herculean problems in operations because of top-heavy executive ranks. There is now some evidence of a retreat from further finely drawn distinctions in titles and executive status symbols. The companies are scratching desperately for some new gimmick to jazz up their executive personnel.

Pay Him More than Enough

It is a severe shock to large companies to discover now and again that a man they want to "attract" to their employ is already earning as much as, or more than, they are willing to pay. This is particularly true of key men working for progressive, growing, medium-sized companies. Top management of these companies is completely aware of the value of good executives in building or expanding their share of the market. Their key men are frequently overpaid in relation to the salary scales of large companies.

Top management generally is learning the hard lesson that it is false thrift to economize on salaries of key men. Questions and criticism from the floor are convincing them that their stockholders realize this too. But in an era of high taxes, it has become increasingly difficult to translate their new wisdom into tangible bene- fit to their executives. The temporary palliative media of profit-sharing, bonus, stock option and other incentive plans has proved only a partial answer.

Taxwise compensation plans are obviously best where the executive or his family receive payment for the executive's present services on a tax-deferred basis . . . that is, taxed only when received . . . and where such payments are actually made at the time most suitable to the executive or his family (on his disability, retirement or death). But companies must steel themselves to set up such plans even if they don't receive the benefit of the now-recognized-as-essential ingredient of a present tax deduction for the company. Here is an area where top management needs specialized advice to avoid putting unnecessary and irrational ceilings on the benefits afforded under such plans. Without such advice, tailored to the circumstances of the company and its executive personnel, top management may bungle its executives and their families out of worthwhile future monetary benefits, rob the company of excellent executives who won't remain very long under such economically restricting bounds, and discourage acquisition of new executive talent for the short or long period the company may require such services.

Life insurance plans purchased by the company have likewise proved of little value to the executives who must pay a tax on the premiums *given* to them. Executives rightly feel they would be better off if given the pay increase (taxable at the same rate) and left to provide their own life insurance protection . . . a matter they feel themselves entirely competent to arrange to their own satisfaction. Annuity plans usually suffer from the same pernicious tax implications.

Nor are executives noticeably intrigued by the promise of "adequate" payments to be made voluntarily by the company in the event of disability or death of the executive. Such promises (as executives well know) are extremely elastic, may be withdrawn at any time, either individually or universally. Why add this tension and stress to the executive's already well-stacked pile of emotional and mental burdens? . . . always assuming, of course, that astute executives would find such an arrangement attractive in the first instance.

Detailed examination of many "plans" now current in industry, including nonqualifying trusts, finds them neither practical nor feasible in successful retention of qualified executive personnel. Some consultants are now advising consideration of a modified trust, which gives the company no deduction for the extra incentive pay provided for executives. Another current and more feasible recommendation is that the company and its executive embark upon mutually beneficial contracts: the company provides for deferment of a stated portion of the executive's income to later income years, commencing with disability, retirement or death—payments to continue at a fixed rate for a fixed period. In return, the executive agrees that the plan be tied to the condition that it will become operative only if the executive contracts to continue in the company's employ until such disability, retirement or death occurs. This contingency is favorable to both parties: the company assures itself both of tax deduction and of proven executive talent; the executive is assured of deferred (and perhaps canceled) taxation on part of his income when he begins to collect it in future years, thus is willing to accept the contingency which at first blush may seem unpalatable or restrictive.

Whether this mutual contingency agreement, or still another variation of the deferred compensation idea, can be made a valuable part of the company's compensation package for executives is a matter fully warranting top management's closest attention.

Give Him a "Human" Boss

No one should understand better than his boss the price a man must pay to become a good executive. He should understand and sympathize because he himself has paid in the same coin: the inner tensions and frustrations, the emotional strain of having to succeed despite an ever-present fear of failure or losing ground, the disappointments, the sense of insecurity and loneliness.

Watching your subordinate struggle to learn self-discipline and tolerance, you will remember all too readily your own difficulties— and how many anxious hours you could have been spared had *you* had a perceptive, generous superior. How much does it cost to be "human," approachable, helpful?

When you see your subordinate going stale, for example, getting bogged down in a dreary routine which saps his enthusiasm, dulls his mind and emotions—how simple it is for you to change his horizons. Assign him temporarily to a different job. It may be the same uninspiring work, actually, as his original assignment. But it's a change, a break in the work pattern—perhaps he deals with different people or with different departments in the new assignment. It may be all he needs to refresh his zeal and interest.

Or it may be possible to set up a project which will have him working with stimulating associates he rarely has an opportunity to brush minds with. Measuring himself against men of such caliber will effectively enlarge his view of himself, correct his perspectives.

Other suggestions will occur to you, once you begin: a book he might find interesting; an organization he should join because of the stimulating contacts it would afford him, an introduction to people outside the company he might find rewarding to cultivate.

Such attention on your part to your subordinate's unexpressed, perhaps unarticulated, needs demonstrates to him as nothing else can that you are sincerely interested in him and in his job happiness. It proves to him that you value him sufficiently to invest your time, thoughts and loyalty in his behalf. This kind of warm and sincere interest on the part of supervising management is sadly so rare in the business environment that even a slight manifestation of its existence evokes an almost fanatical loyalty in the fortunate subordinate.

Incidentally, this problem of executive "staleness" is receiving increasing attention by thoughtful management. In one company, for example, an effort is being made to break plaster-cast thinking habits and outlooks by sending management people away for one week each year. The group is accommodated at a good quiet hotel "in the country." The company secures the services of university lecturers, well-known authors, management consultants and professional men. Each conducts an informal forum on an interesting topic, preferably *not* connected with business activities. The men have dinner with a different group each night, spend the evening in discussion and doing "homework." They have a certain amount of "free" time in which to enjoy the hotel's facilities. Reporting on results, the company quotes the men unanimously agreed that the most obvious benefit is relief from tension and pressure. Most of them find something new and interesting to mull over. All welcome the opportunity to get better acquainted with men in the management group they rarely contact in daily operations. The company is convinced of the value of the "week," however slightly it may dent entrenched executive thought patterns.

Down with Luncheon Conferences!

Management people have long since recognized that it isn't necessary to stop working just because it's time for lunch. It's the rare executive who goes to lunch with no purpose except to eat. He hasn't time for such nonsense! Why not take along Bill or Pete —or better still, both: that will mean two fewer meetings that afternoon.

It's only a short step from this innocuous practice to the luncheon conference which has now, like Coca Cola, become part of Americana. It seems almost illegal to have plain conferences these days. Who would attend? Up and down the country, executive calendars are crowded with four or five luncheon conferences a week. What happens? A dozen or more management men, consultants, perhaps customers meet somewhere inconvenient to everybody. (This is helpful, of course, because it takes another half-hour or so from each man's too-short day for travel, usually at the height of the rush hour.) The lunch may be good, or it may not. (Each man can get an excellent lunch within walking distance of his office.) It usually takes at least an hour and a half (drinks, large group to serve, etc.). Then the conference. Either there's no agenda (let's keep it informal), or the agenda is hopelessly overloaded (so that it's only half-covered or discussed sketchily). Halfway through, men begin to fidget (look at the time); they half-listen while they worry about the work waiting for them back in the office. There's no real communication or stimulus—the supposed raisons d'etre for such conferences. When they're over, the men rush back to the office, feeling dissatisfied with the lack of accomplishment, resentful over the increased stress and pressure they are experiencing to "make up" for the extra time taken by the conference. Think this is an exaggerated picture? You're either lucky or lying.

As a matter of fact, so little is accomplished at these luncheon conferences that executives are now going into dinner conferences. Interesting development. Having loused up most of the executive's day, let's louse up most of his evening. Better still, we can add home stress to job stress, really do a job on him!

Since luncheon (or dinner) conferences are now inextricably ensconced in the business scene, let's get them back in the groove. All it takes is adoption and adherence to two rules:

1.   Set a maximum length of time for the conference—*and stick to it*. For most such conferences, two hours is plenty of time.

2.   Set up a plan or program—and see that its purpose is accomplished.

Let's say the conference is scheduled for twelve to two. Give the folks time for one drink (if necessary for conviviality; many executives would as soon do without at such meetings); then get lunch on the table promptly. Keep the introduction of the guest dignified but brief (you can expatiate on his qualifications and achievements in the preconference announcements; don't waste conference time on them). Make the questions brief and provocative (rephrasing as much as necessary) and cut off pointless debate. At two o'clock, *end the meeting.*

With such a policy, conference attendance and conferees' interest will rise sharply. So will the amount of business transacted.

Keep Him Hearty

The same top management which has been sternly educated by the distaff side of the family to treat domestic bric-a-brac with deepest respect, care and devotion, does almost nothing to protect the company life line: the enterprise bric-a-brac known as executive personnel. Does the costliness and irreplaceability of Staffordshire or Dresden exceed the costliness and irreplaceability of management talent?

Even though they have suffered sudden or repeated losses of key men to disabling illness or death, few companies are doing anything about protecting the health of their executive group. Here and there, a company has announced establishment of an "Executive Health Program." On closer study, however, these "programs" are found to consist of a yearly medical check-up, provided the executive cares to coöperate. If he doesn't—nothing.

In most companies which have such "programs," the company bears the cost of examination. A uniform arrangement is followed for conducting the examinations—outside clinic; private physician of company's choice; the company's own medical department. Examination includes routine physical examination, blood count and blood chemistry, urinalysis, electrocardiogram, chest x-ray, fluoroscopic examination, serological blood test. A very few companies include a psychiatric interview within the scope of the examination.

Some companies require information on the examination findings to be transmitted to them; others do not ask for the findings, instead have them sent to the executive's personal physician.

As a preventive health program, this is obviously inadequate. To begin with, *all* executives must be participants. But most men will feel that the company has no right to information on their medical status in such exhaustive detail—it is still unsettled at which point the executive's right to privacy must give away to the company's right to knowledge of his work abilities. However that point is finally settled, it is obvious that executives will coöperate to a larger extent if the company carries the cost of the examinations but respects the executive's privacy. All the company wants to accomplish, actually, is to have incipient trouble detected and corrected. It isn't necessary for the company to know whether a latent condition is actually discovered. Why not provide instead that the report of examination be sent to the executive's personal physician —to be followed up by him with the executive? The company will have to depend on the attending physician to pass along information he thinks the company should have. This necessarily implies that the company must develop good relations with the executive's physician, not only to facilitate carrying out the preventative examinations, but also to pressure the executive to take care of any situation which may be discovered, without procrastination.

It would be preferable to have the executive examination performed by rotating panels of consultants, who examine with the benefit of the man's medical file. This will help prevent familiarity with the man's condition from causing the examiner to overlook developing conditions. There should be a complete work-up yearly, but also spot checks every three months. Any difficulty which may be uncovered must be handled by the executive and his personal physician, but the physician has the support of the company behind his recommendations, should that be necessary.

Suppose the company wants to do the program with its own people. First, it has to provide the facilities for the examinations. It can do this in its own medical department, provided the department is properly set up for the diagnostic tests, x-rays, etc. If not (as will be true in most companies), those will have to be done "outside."

Also, it will have to refer executives to outside consultants for at least the one exhaustive medical examination each year. The reports from these outside examinations will then have to be coördinated and evaluated by its medical director and a finalized report prepared.

Another method would be for the company to make use of hospital or clinic facilities. Most hospitals will require use of their staff people to make the examinations and tests; others will permit use of outside consultants in conjunction with their staff specialists.

There is also a third method: The company could use a private setup with a private practitioner (rather than hospital or clinic). The private physician then arranges for outside consultation as necessary, and he prepares the final report.

Having made a choice of method for providing the required examinations, the company must decide how to handle the findings. A recent survey shows that about one-third of the companies required a report of the examination to be submitted to them. In a company-controlled setup, this would mean deciding whether the report should be labeled "confidential"—held in the medical department and not available for reference except on permission given by the executive. It would mean also making special provision for typing and handling of such reports if "leaks" are not to occur.

Although labeled "confidential," the file is there—subject to change of policy at any time. There is almost universal agreement that where medical information is available, it influences decisions on advancement, and unfairly so at times. Where several men were being considered for a higher post, for example, one was eliminated from further consideration because of a diabetic condition—although it had existed for ten years, was clearly under control and had never caused a day's absence. Fair or not, therefore, such happenings influence the executive's attitude toward examinations by the company medical department.

As for frequency: The program envisions one really tiptop thorough-going medical examination each year, with all the diagnostic tests considered valuable, plus any others which may be indicated on the basis of the findings. The program also envisions a follow-up check, six months later. This is minimum. Of course where defects are found, the executive should be under his physician's care and be seen by him as often as necessary.

Maintaining a diary: In a company-administered program, a diary must be maintained to make sure examinations are given as scheduled. This means assigning to a secretary the awkward and embarrassing job of dogging the company's top executives with the repeated request that they please go see the doctor.

Costs? Well, in a company-administered program, it will mean setting up new procedures, assigning new duties to some people, perhaps hiring extra people. Computing actual costs will mean putting an army of cost accountants to work on the records. It may also mean placing a heavy onus on the chief of your company's medical department—making him ineffective in other duties of the medical division.

The problems which companies have encountered in attempting to set up and maintain their own voluntary executive health programs have raised the question whether an outside program or service might be preferable. Industrial and commercial associations have been actively investigating whether they could be helpful in this area. The idea would be to have an executive health service run by the association on a subscription basis. Companies would pay for the subscriptions of all their executives, at a fixed fee per executive. The fee would provide each executive with a complete initial physical examination at a designated center convenient to the company's location. Six or eight such centers, centrally located, would be set up across the country. These centers would be equipped with the latest and best diagnostic devices and staffed by a panel of top-flight specialists expressly selected for this service. The report of this first exhaustive examination would be sent to the executive's private physician for follow-up. He would be expected to call the executive in for an interview sometime during the month following the examination. The service would maintain a tickler system on its subscribers, and routinely call the executive back once more during the year following. The cost is estimated at $75–$150 per executive. Reports of these spot checks would be sent to the executive's private physician. At the end of a year, another thorough-going examination, with laboratory work, etc., would be given. None of the medical information disclosed in the examinations would be given to the executive's employer. It would be assumed that should a condition be disclosed which might interfere with performance of his duties, the executive himself would see to it that the necessary information was given to the company.

By participating in an outside executive health service of this type, the company would achieve several objectives. First, it would prove to the executive that it sincerely wanted to be helpful in its avowed desire to see to it that his health was protected. Second, it would respect the executive's right to privacy as to his health situation while insuring that he did not abuse that right by neglecting protective measures for his health. Third, the company could avoid assuming the added burden of further administrative work involved in every new "program" or service which a company adopts for the benefit of its employees. Fourth, placing the program in the hands of an outside group provides a measure of control and discipline over the executive which the company itself might fail to receive and hesitate to demand. Finally, as in all other types of insurance, the cost to the company of such a service would be far less than would be the case if it tried to provide the same quality of medical attention on its own.

It seems a safe bet that executive health service programs, along the lines now being explored, will find a ready market and fill a real need.

This, however, is still only preventative protection. Top management has a more active role to perform in protection of its valuable executive group: to do everything possible in the business environment to relieve the killing pressures on the man's time and central nervous system. The wealth of "health-saving" suggestions on rerouting of his workload which followed a recent Presidential heart attack is instructive. Nothing can be done to take the load of responsibility off an executive's back—but that's not what harries him to early disability or death. Rather, it's the constant race against the clock which leaves him limp and exhausted at the end of his work day. Almost always, it is only top management which can do anything constructive about executive-killing schedules and pressures. Take just one small example: executive vacations. Our interviews have disclosed that only 30% of the executives we spoke to could count on having an undisturbed vacation of more than 11 days. Most men admitted that they had "working" vacations—made up of tightly planned schedules of so-called leisure heavily interlarded with business appointments or projects to which they were devoting most of their "resting" time. Does the company worry about this situation? Far from it—as a matter of fact, it encourages it by its own actions. Consider, for example, the college management training courses it wants its people to take. Many of them are summer courses, held on a beautiful campus. They are billed as part work, part leisure, with facilities for sports and time to indulge them. In fact, they are "all work and tension," in the words of one recent student who wanted to know what kind of golf he could be expected to play with his mind whirling with new "horizons and fresh outlooks." When management encourages the executive to take such a course as his so-called "vacation," it neatly adds another problem to the executive's well-loaded shoulders: domestic discord. Executives' wives can hardly be expected to greet with joy the prospect of spending several weeks on a college campus—virtually alone—with husbands who are as much (or more) distracted and tense as they are at home.

Or consider another example of management's own responsibility in this area: vacations for newly hired executives. The company spends unstintingly to canvass the field, investigate and hire good men to fill executive posts. It then suddenly starts pinching pennies. Company policy says an employee must have certain minimum service to qualify for paid vacation. Therefore, this executive—whose recruitment has probably cost the company $10,000 to $15,000—is now suddenly not valuable enough to be worth several hundred dollars in technically unearned vacation. Preposterous? No, just the usual practice.

Obviously, there is no substitute for a well-planned vacation: well-planned, that is, by the executive himself without regard to his job requirements or pressures. A top management which does not recognize this fact—and insist on such a vacation for each of its valuable executives *each year*—is obviously in its infancy so far as realistic attention to conservation of executive health is concerned.

Give Him Good Consultants

Progressively complicated needs arise and increase as results of the conflicting forces arising throughout our industrial scheme. Whereas, earlier, the middleman, the broker, the agent, the intermediate merchant was available for conference and advice, business by its bigness has shunted aside such aides. Out of the new and greater needs has emerged the role of management consultants.

It is not a simple routine to unravel and unwrap the multiple layers of poor managerial behavior and its accompanied rationalization masking the core of realistic facts in a company's poor competitive position. Sincere consultants can aid you in *your* accomplishment of getting at the facts and altering the company's position without dramatic or gaudily gilt-packaged cure-alls. Such aid is not clothed in unrestrained enthusiasm for all that is *new* and scorn for all that is *old*. Neither is it steeped in complicated procedures calculated to perpetuate the need for aid.

More and more, today, testing is made the whole as against a mere descriptive part of not only appraisal or evaluation, but of the very maintenance of the executive team. New and more cleverly devised tests appear in great profusion, each with its proponents enthusiastically proclaiming results. What results? More and bigger filing cabinets? More time wasted by already harried executives now forced to practice a decerebrate ritual of forms, forums, multi-colored charts and generously spiraled graphs?

Such overly enthusiastic proponents, obviously of the belief that great business enterprise can function with no independent thinking at all, are not true consultants. If sincere, their myopic approach cannot be helpful. If lacking a sincere interest in easing the burden of the executive team or in aiding the advance of willing candidates, they can exercise vicious effects by their "services"—effects reflected in the disappointment and shaken confidence of the very management team itself. Consider the impact on subordinates who look to the management team for support and who are greeted, instead, with more forms, more ritual, more hocus-pocus, and less time to do what they *know* must be done.

Choosing a good consultant is not a matter of finding a name in the telephone directory. The largest firm in your area may not be the best for your purposes. Many consultants specialize in one or another aspect of business operations. For example, some consultants act as "super" employment agencies—work exclusively in recruitment of men to fill clients' executive-level positions. Such a consultant will find the candidates, put them through the testing routine, send the client a report on men who seem suitable.

Services of this type of specialist consultant are most efficiently employed where management already knows what the problem is, merely needs assistance in solving it. For example, a company plans to build a new plant. The problem is where to locate it. Rather than lose the services of several of its key people to do the necessary research, planning, supervising, coördinating, the company may find it preferable to bring in a consultant firm which specializes in engineering problems. The firm will suggest and survey possible plant sites, provide up-to-the-minute information on the newest industrial plant designs, relieve management as much as possible of the detail work involved when construction starts.

However, where management does not have a specific problem, it needs the services of a consultant who can supply a fresh, broad viewpoint on overall operations. It needs a consultant who can work on a continuing basis with the management group, providing suggestions or making recommendations in every area of operations.

Choosing your management consultant may be more important in the long run than choosing your accountant or your lawyer—because of the long-range and permanent implications the consultant has upon your valuable executive personnel.

An important principle of pathology may be used effectively in our analysis of the Executive Floor. There are two factors in the development of any morbid process: first, the agent initiating damage to tissue; and second, the pathological reaction thereby set in motion. The attractive window dressing of many still pending executive development programs have already initiated damage to the vital tissue of the Executive Floor. The reaction in these instances has been continued poor performance; loss of confidence in individual executives; and either nonformation, malformation, or disintegration of the executive team.

Many present "packages" of executive development carry with them an ever-hungry search for the "aggressive" executive: men who rate their gains as nothing in contrast to their ever-receding goals; men who must dominate, and, by domination, control; hostile men who are best suited to the prize ring and not to industry and the management of a labor force growing increasingly aware of its own power and potential; men who ruin executive team play by limiting too narrowly the circle within which power is confined; who increase the impact of the clouds and cobwebs of the mind by the use of closed-circuit TV to "communicate" and, thereby, to manage. Lust for movement and fair acquisition, accompanied as it is with buoyant style and mental flair, should not be miscalled "aggressive."

Throughout this study of the behavior pattern representing the executive in action, we have endeavored to view not only the executive and his job—but their relationship to the whole of management. Our inquiry has admittedly led us into some highly sensitive, intensely controversial areas. One finding is incontestable. Respect for others—in and out of management—is the distinguishing characteristic of successful executive performance. And, such appreciative consideration of the value of the contributions of others can only be a by-product of self-respect based upon enlightened self-discipline.

The tremendous growth of industry has created problems, but each great stride has been marked by progress—a way that has seen the rise of funded altruism that is and has become a target for political headline hunters. Such enlargement of the sphere of world sympathy and happiness; such recognition of the place and value of the social instincts have come as direct products of past executive skill. Let us borrow from it deeply in accomplishment of the goals ahead.

Addenda

For the Chart-Minded

Evaluations need not be on a form or chart basis. For those whose minds are impressed more vividly by the use of symbols or the visual evidence of forms, charts and graphs, these are suggested—only as implements if believed necessary. The human mind and heart are much too complex, much too wonderful to be reduced to such common denominators. The inner ticking that goes into the he or she who makes a good executive cannot and should not be subjected to rejection or acceptance on the basis of "cold" graphic display. When used as a tool, a form, chart, or graph can be of value.

The following are examples of *reminders* which may prove useful to an appraiser of managerial talent in terms of position classification, capacities essential and the abilities available. These generally should not be used as is, but adapted to suit the company's peculiar needs or characteristics.

Job Profile

The use of a job profile as a management tool in evaluation of men and positions is discussed in detail in Chapter IV.

JOB PROFILE

Name of Employee:
Present Level:
Next Level:

Needs Improvement for
Present Level:
Next Level:

Ability Needed

Public Contacts
National and International Economics

MANAGER

Planning
Organization
Sales
Legislation

ASSISTANT MANAGER

Community Problems
Public Relations
Labor Relations

DIVISION SUPERVISOR

Operations
Transportation
Employee Communications

ASSISTANT DIVISION SUPERVISOR

Policies
Procedures
Budget
Materials

DEPARTMENT HEAD

JOB PROFILE

Executive: OFFICE MANAGER

RESPONSIBILITY:	PER CENT OF TIME						
	0	10	20	30	40	50	60
Planning		x					
Cöordination			x				
Preparing Procedures and Methods		x					
Interpreting Directives and Practices		x					
Supervising Operations	x						
Personnel Activities					x		
Public Relations		x					
Consultation		x					
Negotiations	x						
Scheduling	x						
Preparing Reports	x						
Evaluation		x					

Date:

JOB PROFILE

Executive: VICE PRESIDENT

RESPONSIBILITY:	PER CENT OF TIME						
	0	10	20	30	40	50	60
Planning			x				
Cöordination		x					
Preparing Procedures and Methods	x						
Interpreting Directives and Practices		x					
Supervising Operations	x						
Personnel Activities		x					
Public Relations					x		
Consultation		x					
Negotiations	x						
Scheduling	x						
Preparing Reports	x						
Evaluation		x					

Date:

Evaluation Forms

The use of a form as a management tool in evaluation of management people, their performance and potential, is discussed in detail in Chapter IV. These two samples may be useful in developing your own form.

SUGGESTED EVALUATION FORM NO. 1

Employee: Title:
Appraised by: Date:

SUMMARY OF RATINGS

_____ Vision   _____ Drive and Enthusiasm
_____ Interpersonal Relations   _____ Administrative and
_____ Initiative and Adaptability   Supervisory Ability
_____ Judgment and Job   _____ Ambition
        Knowledge

Insert:

A—if you mean Excellent, Superior, Very High, Far Above Average
B—if you mean Very Good, Above Average
C—if you mean Good, Satisfactory, Average
D—If you mean Poor, Unsatisfactory, Much Below Average

Check below the employee's performance in relation to the requirements of his post.

To What Extent:	Always	Very Often	Some-times	Never

VISION

Does he bring new ideas about his post to his superior?

| | ——— | ——— | ——— | ——— |

Does he, within good organization practice, bring to his superior new ideas about other areas in the business (sales, design or engineering, manufacturing, personnel, controls, public relations)?

| | ——— | ——— | ——— | ——— |

Are his ideas practical?

| | ——— | ——— | ——— | ——— |

INTERPERSONAL RELATIONS

Does he stimulate his associates and subordinates to higher levels of performance?

| | ——— | ——— | ——— | ——— |

Does he succeed in selling ideas and company policies?

| | ——— | ——— | ——— | ——— |

Does he encourage his associates and subordinates by giving credit where credit is deserved?

| | ——— | ——— | ——— | ——— |

Is he tactful in dealing with others at all levels?

| | ——— | ——— | ——— | ——— |

Does he have the confidence and respect of his subordinates and associates?

| | ——— | ——— | ——— | ——— |

Is he personally acceptable to his subordinates and associates?

| | ——— | ——— | ——— | ——— |

	Always	Very Often	Some- times	Never

INITIATIVE AND ADAPTABILITY

Does he, upon seeing a need, do something about it without having to be told?	___	___	___	___
Is he impatient of unnecessary delay?	___	___	___	___
Is he impatient of necessay delays?	___	___	___	___
Does he solicit and adopt the good ideas of others and put them into effective operation?	___	___	___	___

JUDGMENT AND JOB KNOWLEDGE

Does he consider and interpret correctly all the important facts in solving a problem?	___	___	___	___
In his overall knowledge adequate for his job?	___	___	___	___
Is he successful in avoiding costly mistakes?	___	___	___	___
Does he make decisions promptly?	___	___	___	___
Does he squarely accept responsibility for his decisions—especially those which prove to be wrong?	___	___	___	___
Does he learn and profit from his experience?	___	___	___	___
Does he learn and profit from the experience of others?	___	___	___	___

	Always	Very Often	Some- times	Never

DRIVE AND ENTHUSIASM

	Always	Very Often	Some-times	Never
Does he apply personal energy and enthusiasm to see a thing through despite obstacles?	___	___	___	___
Does he inspire subordinates to do so?	___	___	___	___
Does he persevere in each assignment until it is completed or the objective is reached?	___	___	___	___

ADMINISTRATIVE AND SUPERVISORY ABILITY

	Always	Very Often	Some-times	Never
Does he organize his work to get desired results?	___	___	___	___
Does he coördinate and work effectively with others in the organization?	___	___	___	___
Does he delegate proper responsibility and authority?	___	___	___	___
Does he select good subordinates?	___	___	___	___
Does he train people well?	___	___	___	___
Does he objectively review and accurately appraise the performance of his subordinates?	___	___	___	___

AMBITION

State briefly:

Where does he want to be 10 years from now?

Where does he want to be 5 years from now?

What special preparation has he made outside of his job experience for the goal for which he is aiming?

What special preparation is he now making in the way of outside studies, associations or experience?

Is his goal a realistic one or is it beyond his capacity?

Are his inherent capabilities such that he should be encouraged to the attainment of his goal?

Is there any condition either of a business, personal or other nature, which would limit his flexibility for advancement or relocation? Explain:

What help can his supervisors give him toward the education and experience necessary to round out what he already has?

Summarizing your answers to these questions, check below your appraisal of this man's capacity for advancement to a position of greater responsibility.

1. POTENTIAL FOR ADVANCEMENT (possesses capacity to assume greater responsibility)

   a._____ Can be considered immediately promotable to a position in the next level of responsibility.

   b._____ Can be considered capable of assuming greater responsibility after training.

2. DOUBTFUL CAPACITY FOR ADVANCEMENT

   a._____ Performing satisfactorily on this job and well suited to it but probably more suited to this work or similar responsibility than to a position of greater responsibility.

   b._____ Inadequate performance. Performance in present assignment is below standard and/or lacks ability to meet standards of performance for such assignment.

ACTION RECOMMENDED:

SUGGESTED EVALUATION FORM NO. 2

Instructions:

The care and accuracy with which this appraisal is made will determine its value to you, to the employee, and to the organization. It should reflect a sound and impartial judgment of the employee's performance on currently assigned responsibilities.

Reference to the employee's position or job description will help you in making a realistic analysis, based upon actual job requirements and performance.

Consider each *factor* separately and independently. Your entries in the columns should be indicated by placing a check mark under the appropriate heading. Space is provided for brief narrative comment.

	Excellent	Superior	Marginal	Poor
ABILITY TO DELEGATE AUTHORITY. The assigning of appropriate duties and power to subordinates to develop and execute their designated duties.	——	——	——	——
ABILITY TO DEVELOP ASSISTANTS. Arouse subordinates' interests and ambitions, alleviating their weaknesses through counsel and guidance.	——	——	——	——
ABILITY TO PLAN AND CONTROL. The ability to provide a logical, effective course of action, and follow through to see that objectives are achieved.	——	——	——	——
COÖPERATION. The ability to deal successfully with people, by willingness and capacity to work harmoniously with subordinates or superiors.	——	——	——	——

	Excel- lent	Su- perior	Margi- nal	Poor
HEALTH AND VITALITY. Mental and physical endurance (based upon your observation and knowledge).	___	___	___	___
IMAGINATION AND ORIGINALITY. The ability to anticipate changing needs and conditions, conceive new creative ideas or procedures.	___	___	___	___
INITIATIVE. The ability to act independently without specific instructions in a poised, self-confident, eager manner.	___	___	___	___
JUDGMENT. The ability to arrive at sound, logical opinions on available data.	___	___	___	___
KNOWLEDGE. A clear understanding of those facets which are pertinent to the employee's post.	___	___	___	___
SELF-EXPRESSION. Clear, effective, oral or written presentations.	___	___	___	___
STABILITY UNDER PRESSURE. Mental and emotional balance under stress; no interference by home problems.	___	___	___	___
TRUSTWORTHINESS AND RELIABILITY. Conscientious, thorough, perseverant.	___	___	___	___

COMMENT IN NARRATIVE FORM ON THESE POINTS:

What is your overall evaluation of the employee's performance, summarizing the entries made above?

What is your current estimate of this employee's capacity and ambition for future growth?

What needs to be said about any particular strengths or weaknesses?

OVERALL COMMENTS:

What does this employee have to say about how he is getting along with his work, his associates and with you?

Where does the employee believe he might, in the future, serve himself and the company best—and why?

ACTION TO BE TAKEN: TIME TABLE:

Prepared by: Date:

Forced Choice Questionnaire

This sample of a Forced Choice Questionnaire developed in one company may help you in devising your own if it seems indicated because appraisers of executive personnel are not doing a pinpointed job. Chapter IV discusses in detail the application of this technique to help appraisers to appraise fairly and perceptively.

FORCED CHOICE QUESTIONNAIRE

Employee's Name: Title:
Department: Time in Position:

INSTRUCTIONS: Kindly read each of the following groups of statements carefully. Decide which statement is best descriptive of the employee's performance. Check the statement you have selected; be sure to select only one from each group of three statements.

_____ Highly respected for fair play

_____ Quick to grasp information passed on to him

_____ Willingly volunteers assistance to fellow supervisors

_____ Makes the best of his opportunities

_____ Readily adaptable to new situations

_____ Calmly discusses problems with his people

_____ Coöperates with his associates

_____ Has fine standards of personal conduct

_____ Respects authority and plant policies

_____ Doesn't get brittle under tension

_____ Gets good results from his people

_____ Always backs up his subordinates

_____ Has good judgment

_____ Does a good job of presenting material in written form

_____ The men know that they can rely on his conclusions

_____ Has a wide background of experience

_____ His men as well as men not supervised by him have confidence in him

_____ Isn't afraid of his boss

_____ He is ready to give credit to others for good work done

_____ Knows when to exercise his authority and when not to

_____ Holds his people accountable for doing their work in the approved manner

---

_____ Respected by all fellow supervisors

_____ Teamwork exists among his men

_____ Works best under stress

_____ Very well informed on all phases of his work

_____ Dependable under all circumstances

_____ Well-liked by associates

_____ Participates in staff discussions

_____ Accepts responsibility of each job

_____ Well-liked by superiors

_____ Easygoing

_____ Modest and reserved

_____ Plays no favorites

_____ Has a good sense of humor

_____ Is generally enthusiastic

_____ Thoughtful of others

_____ Well-liked by subordinates

_____ Businesslike

_____ Has many friends

_____ Is qualified to handle his job

_____ Plans his work in advance

_____ Has definite job standards

_____ Is not flighty

_____ Puts forth his best effort

_____ Pitches in when going is rough

_____ Keeps his promises

_____ Follows instructions carefully

_____ Is a loyal friend

Sample Job Rotation Schedule

The use of job rotation as a development device in increasing the skills of management people is discussed in detail in Chapter IV. The following sample is taken from a company which uses this device extensively.

JOB ROTATION TRAINING SCHEDULE

Name:
Department:

ASSIGNMENT	Needs No Training	Weeks of Training	Period of Training	Training Completed
Receiving				
Marking				
Shipping				
Unit Buying Control				
Customer Service				
Selling in Various Divisions				
Managing a Soft-Line Division				
Managing a Hard-Line Division				
Operating				
Personnel				
Credit and Collection				
Advertising and Display				
Merchandising and Sales Promotion				

Remarks:

Management Charts

The usefulness of management charts as a tool for management was fully discussed in Chapter VII. The following samples were selected to show the various types in use in industry today. In these charts stars have been used as indicators; in preparing your charts, various color markings may be substituted.

Chart I shows the company's executive positions, the last evaluation of the performance of the men holding the positions, and indicates top-level decisions on the estimated period of time in which action is indicated for each position. This is the type of chart which must be revised after each executive evaluation, or change in executive position, so it will always picture the true status of management personnel in the company.

Chart I   Executive Positions

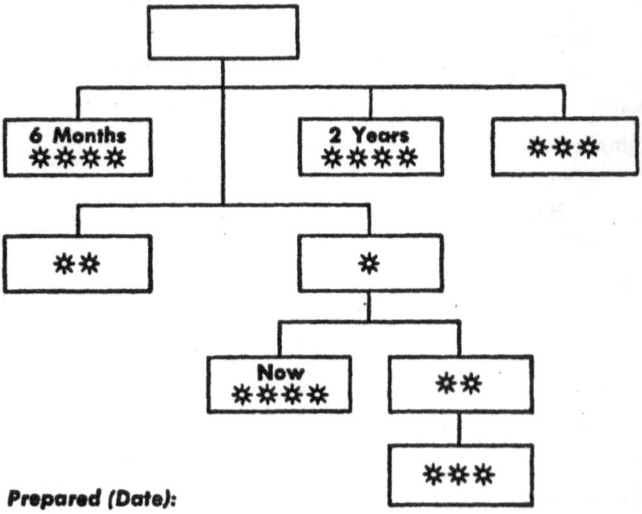

Prepared (Date):

KEY	�֍�֍�֍�֍ Promotable	✶✶ Indefinite
	✶✶✶ Adequate	✶ Unsatisfactory

Looking over Chart I, it is immediately apparent that a serious promotional gap exists at the third management level, where one executive is performing unsatisfactorily, and the other is classed indefinite because he is a new employee, and it is too early to judge his performance. Decisions will have to be made, therefore, on when action should be taken to remedy the gap, and what action. After the changes have been made, a new chart must be drawn up showing the current status of the executive positions and personnel.

A similar type of management chart, Chart II includes the further information of alternate routes for promotion from other units or departments.

Chart II   Future Potential Promotions
Between Units or Departments

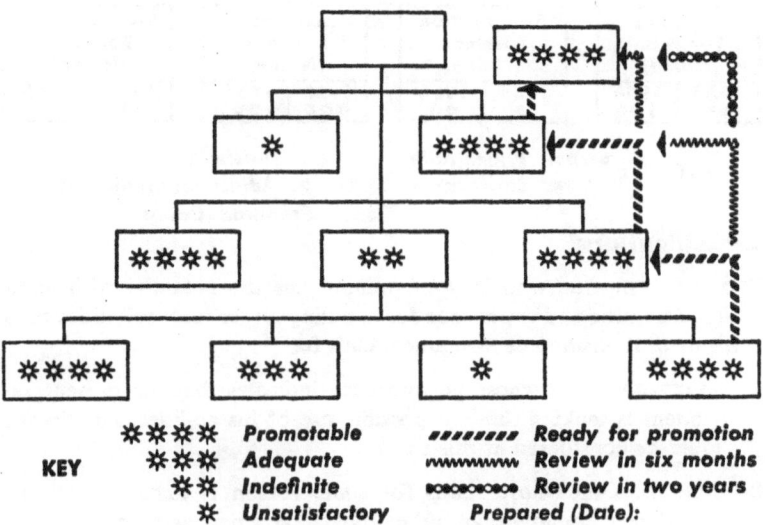

KEY	✳✳✳✳	Promotable	✐✐✐✐✐✐✐	Ready for promotion
	✳✳✳	Adequate	wwwwww	Review in six months
	✳✳	Indefinite	⊶⊶⊶⊶⊶	Review in two years
	✳	Unsatisfactory		Prepared (Date):

Some companies prefer to have the management chart carry cumulative information on appraisals of executives. Each time an appraisal is made, the executive's performance is rated, and shown on the organizational chart with the appropriate date. Thus, on Chart III, not only the executive's performance but also his progress, can be assessed in terms of the entire organization.

Chart III Unit Organization—
Cumulative Performance Appraisal

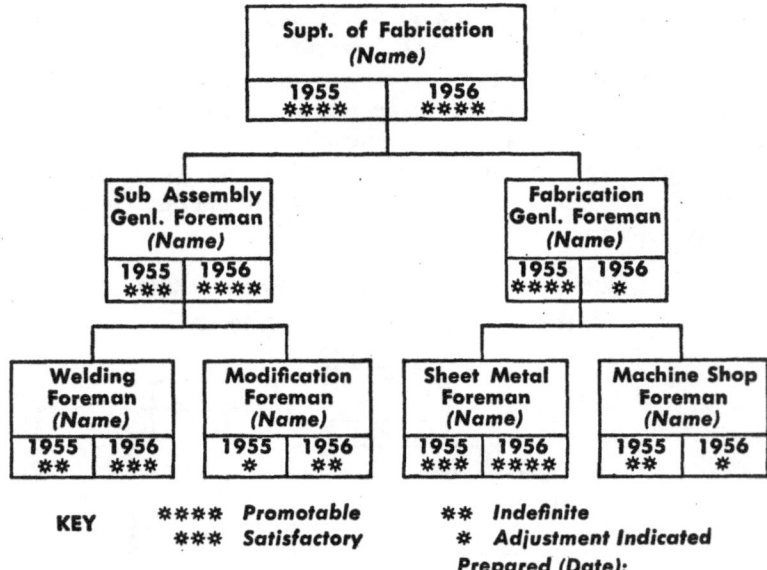

KEY   ✻✻✻✻ *Promotable*   ✻✻ *Indefinite*
        ✻✻✻ *Satisfactory*   ✻ *Adjustment Indicated*
                                  Prepared (Date):

Classifications

PROMOTABLE: One who in your opinion has the potential with additional training and experience for handling larger responsibilities than his present position or assignment calls for.

SATISFACTORY: One whose performance indicates that his present assignment is making the best possible use of his abilities. No change should be considered at this time.

INDEFINITE: One whose status for some reason is uncertain at this time: A new employee, an old employee on a new assignment, or an employee with a special program.

ADJUSTMENT INDICATED: A situation where for some reason management should take action such as an old employee for whom a replacement should be identified and trained; an employee who requires training or personal coaching to improve his performance; or where other action is indicated.

Organizational Charts IV and V show for each executive position not only the current performance of the incumbent, but also that of his possible successor or successors. They are used where the routes for promotion are established, so that successors are known.

Chart IV   General Manufacturing Superintendent

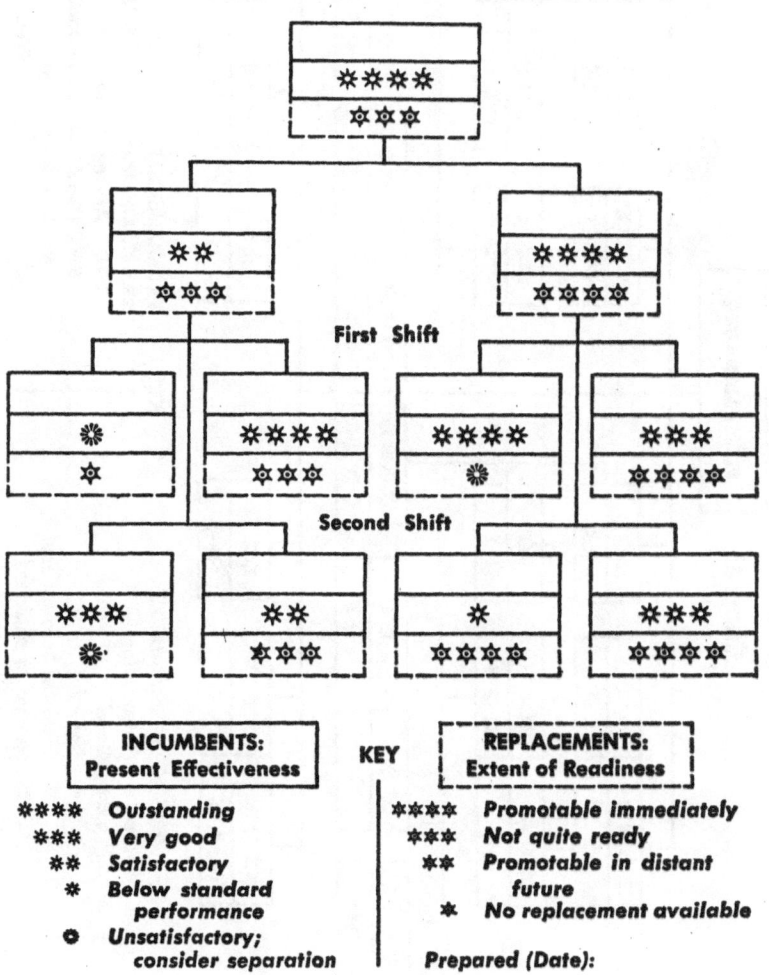

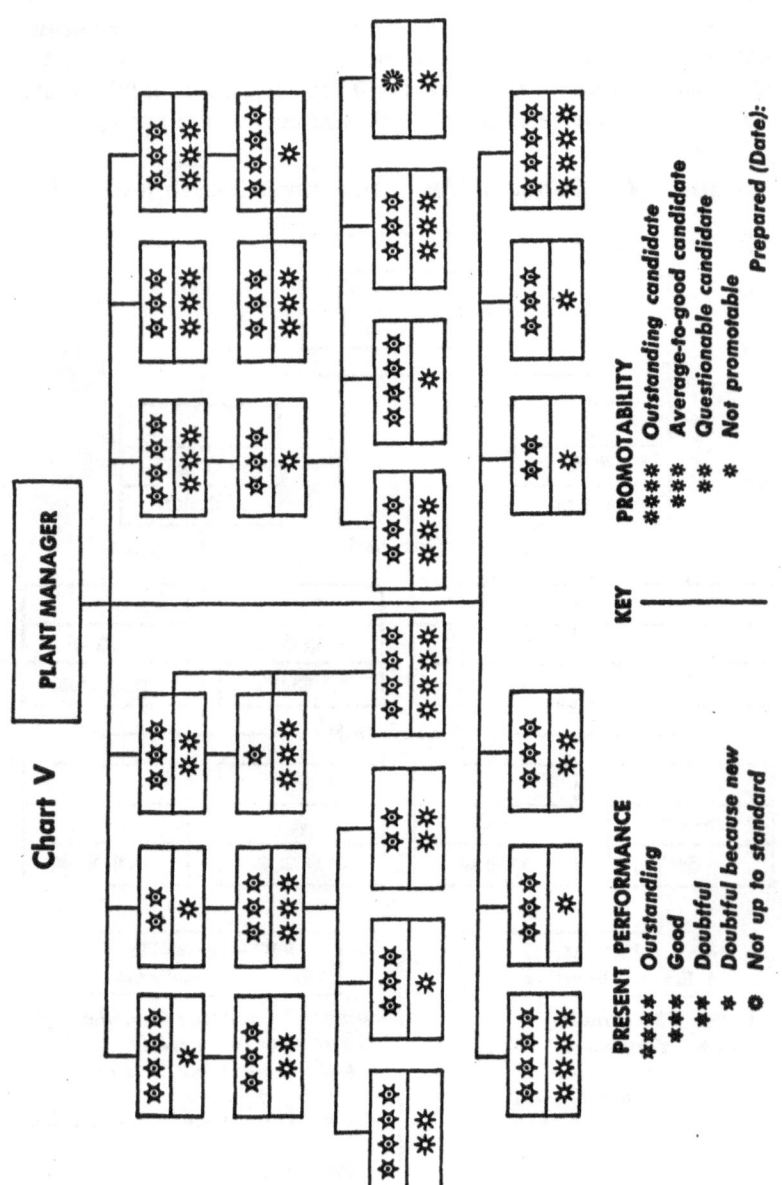

Chart V

PLANT MANAGER

KEY ——————

PRESENT PERFORMANCE
**** Outstanding
*** Good
** Doubtful
* Doubtful because new
⊙ Not up to standard

PROMOTABILITY
**** Outstanding candidate
*** Average-to-good candidate
** Questionable candidate
* Not promotable

Prepared (Date):

If new positions are to be added to the organization, they can also be shown on the organization chart.

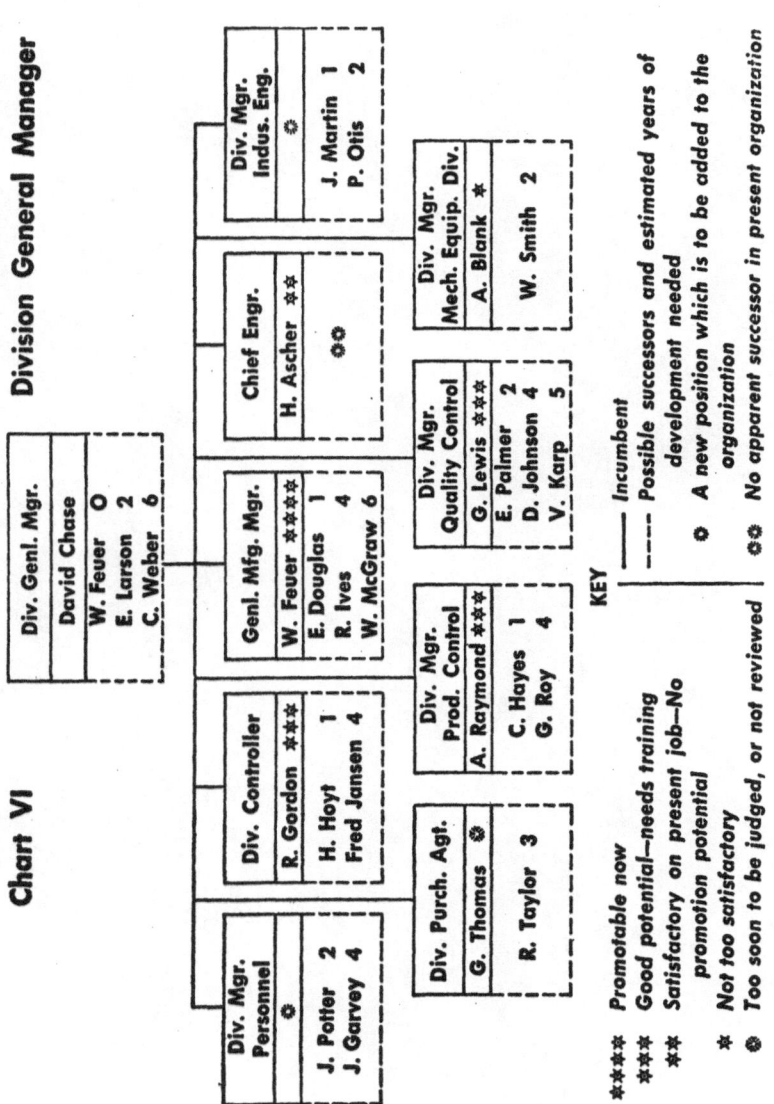

Chart VI — Division General Manager

Back to School

An excellent—and practically painless—method to broaden the scope of management personnel is attendance at university courses which are developed specifically for this purpose. Exposure to the principles and discussions involved in such courses, and contacts with other "promising" management people, can be very helpful in providing new horizons and goals for talented executives. As cautioned in Chapter VI, however, top management should consider such outside courses only as *supplements* to the daily work experience by which executives learn to be executives. No outside course of study can *substitute* for this on-the-job development in which the executive's superiors actively participate, and which is the outgrowth of the company's sincere concern for the growth of its management people.

To help top management know what is available in outside schooling for executive-level personnel, some of the courses presently being offered are discussed below. Fees quoted are for forthcoming sessions, at time of writing. More detailed information may be obtained from the schools mentioned.

University of Buffalo

Its School of Business Administration offers management training programs leading to the degree of Master of Business Administration. Students must have college degree, can complete the course
in two years attending classes two evenings a week, or in three
years attending classes one evening a week. Informal discussion and
actual business cases are used as the method of instruction. Classes
are limited in size, preference is given to men selected and sub-
sidized by their employers. Subjects studied include Business
Economics, Industrial and Human Relations Sequence, Management Controls Sequence ('finance, statistics, accounting), Marketing Sequence; and Business Organization Sequence. Tuition fees
are $19.25 per semester hour.

Two programs are offered: One for men at junior executive
level, who have some years of business experience and whose previous training was in fields other than business administration. It is
intended to bridge the gap between their technical training and the
managerial responsibilities they will assume later. The second program is for graduates of business schools with an undergraduate
degree in business administration or commerce, who want broad
business training at an advanced level. Groups meet separately for
the first year, but meet jointly during the second and third year.

University of California

An Engineering and Management Course at the Los Angeles
campus is intended for presidents, vice-presidents, executives, managers and supervisors; no formal educational requirements are
specified. The course runs from 8:00 A.M. to 5:00 P.M. each day
with four one-and-one-half-hour instruction periods daily plus a
luncheon meeting. Students choose four courses from twenty subjects offered: General Management Principles (engineering and
research administration, economics of plant investment and equipment replacement, managerial adjustment to labor law and union
relations, leadership principles), Traditional Industrial Engineering
(production management principles, integrated manufacturing controls, problems in work measurement and wage payment, factory

layout and material movement, organization and administration of an industrial engineering department), Broad Industrial Techniques (paperwork improvement, work measurement and incentives applied to paper work, laboratory in leadership, industrial statistics and quality control, public speaking), New Techniques (electronic data processing for business, digital computers for industrial users, automation, mathematical bases for decision and programming in industry, industrial operations research). There are also early morning and late afternoon laboratory sessions in public speaking; and two evening meetings with lectures on "dealing with ourselves before dealing with others," and "how to keep from digging your grave while at work."

Fee for the course is $300, covering texts, lunches and two dinners. The course runs for ten days.

The Los Angeles campus also provides an Executive Program in business management. This is a part-time program for middle-management and executive-level personnel, which is focused on general management and does not require the participant to be away from his job. The program supplements the firm's internal executive development work by helping to develop a general management approach to business problems, stimulating the man's desire to improve his ability as a manager, studying the decision-making process, and the cultural, scientific and political factors affecting business operations. Each participant attends two semesters, with a new group beginning each September and each February. If the man's job demands make it impossible for him to stay with the program two consecutive semesters, he can take the second part at a later date. The group meets regularly one day each week, attending two courses, one from 4 to 6 P.M. and the other from 7 to 9 P.M. There is an additional dinner meeting, off campus, which has a featured speaker and includes a discussion period. Outside reading, preparation of cases and report writing are required. No formal examinations or grades. Successful completion of the year's work is recognized with an Executive Program Award. Participants who are accepted for the course are men with responsible positions whose full-time business experience extends over at least five years. Efforts are made to get people from various businesses and from large and small companies. Classes are limited to 50 men. Tuition per semester is $250 plus $50 for meals (which are a required part of the program because of the benefit derived from the informal associations and interchange of ideas made possible by dining together). Both case and text-lecture methods of instruction are used, with emphasis on class participation and discussion.

California Institute of Technology

The Industrial Relations Section offers two one-week Conferences each summer in management development. The course is limited to 22 participants (not more than three from one company at each conference). Participants live on campus, attend morning and afternoon sessions, with evening programs featuring guest speakers, practice in role playing, etc. The fee is $100 for each conference (covers registration and materials).

The University of Chicago

The Executive Program of the School of Business is a two-year evening program of graduate study in business management. It is designed for persons already carrying executive responsibility. It is intended for college graduates but persons with less than four years' college training will be accepted if they have acquired its equivalent informally. Each fall, 75 men are admitted to the program, selection being made on the criteria of whether the man is competent to do graduate work in management, can make substantial contributions to the program from his administrative experience, and exerts an important influence upon enterprise operations. Persons who complete the course satisfactorily receive a certificate; graduates of accredited colleges also receive the degree of Master of Business Administration. The program consists of twelve courses; each course meets once a week from 6:15 to 9:30 P.M. Participants usually take two courses each quarter, move through the program as a unified group. Teaching methods are varied, using both the case and the lecture methods. Reports are required, and reading assignments are made. Tuition is $100 per course; total for two years is $1,200. Subjects include Managerial Accounting, Administrative Relationships, Business Economics, Industry and the Individual, Statistics for Management, Marketing Management, Money and the Financial Markets, Financial Management, Public Regulation of Business, Manufacturing Management, and Theory of Management.

University of Cincinnati

The College of Business Administration offers a course called Advanced Management for Executives which runs each spring and fall for 12 weeks from 2:00 to 4:30 P.M. three days a week. Classes are limited to 20 men, start with a lecture period, end with a round table discussion. No educational prerequisites are made but the student must be recommended by his company and have demonstrated management potential. Topics covered include Policy Making, Administrative Practices, Organizational Procedures, Production, Marketing, Financial Management, Management Controls, and Labor Relations.

Tuition for the course is $275, which covers all expenses except board and lodging.

Columbia University

The Graduate School of Business runs an Executive Program in Business Administration each summer. It is a concentrated six-week course, in two sessions, held at Arden House, Harriman, New York. The program is aimed at men 37–55 years of age. No formal education requirements are made. The first two weeks of the course are spent on determination of business policy; the next two on internal administration; the last two on business management in a dynamic world. The program is limited to 56 men who are already contributing on the policy formulation level and are expected to move into higher managerial positions. Men are selected from a variety of businesses, both large and small, and from different geographic areas to further broaden the value of contacts. Meetings are conducted by questions, informal discussions, group meetings and seminars under the guidance of faculty members, with about three afternoons a week devoted to talks by business, labor and government leaders. Men eat, work and live together. Classes run Monday through Saturday.

Fee for the course is $1,750, including tuition, food and lodging. Companies pay the fee, continue the salary of the students.

Cornell University

The Graduate School of Business offers a six-week course in July-August of each year in the principles, practices and environment of large-scale modern management. It is conducted by the faculty, augmented by prominent executives from business and government. It is aimed at the younger executive in business, with about 10 to 15 years of experience, with a promising future in general management but a background of technical specialization. It is held on the campus, with all participants living at the Executive Development Center there. The course is limited to 30 men. It emphasizes study of Policy Formulation, Organization, Human Relations, Managerial Controls, Political, Economic and Social Trends and Problems, and Top-Management Integration of Forces, Factors and Functions. Fee is $1,200, covers tuition, room and board. The program is planned to supplement techniques commonly used within an organization, and the company is asked to indicate on the application for admission of one of its people, the area or areas of development deemed most desirable for the man.

University of Georgia

An Executive Development Program is held in the summer. It runs for four weeks, classes meeting for four hours each day, with the rest of the time devoted to individual and group study. It is designed for mature executives with 10 to 15 years of experience, at or around the crucial age of 37 to 45 years of age, who have demonstrated their ability to develop as executives and inherent ability to advance in the organization. Program covers Administrative Policy Formulation, Business Management in a Dynamic World, and Human Relations in Management. Members live on the campus in a special building. Instruction is by a variety of participation techniques and the case-study method, with guest speakers, seminars, field trips.

Cost of program is $900, including tuition, texts, room and board. Employers are expected to pay the fees and continue the salary of the members.

(Program members are admitted to the University football team practice; at least one organized dove hunt is scheduled.)

Graduate School of Credit and Financial Management

The school is conducted by the Credit Research Foundation, which is part of the National Association of Credit Men. Sessions are conducted at both Stanford University and at Dartmouth College. The course is designed for mature executives and consists of two-week resident sessions each summer for three summers. The purpose is to develop credit and financial executives to perform their present jobs better and to assume additional managerial responsibilities. Classes are held six days a week. No educational prerequisites, but men must have ten years' business experience in the field of credit and financial management. Students are limited to 200 at Dartmouth; 95 at Stanford. The program of instruction for the first year includes Credit Management, Financial Management I, Development of Executive Abilities, Management Policies and Functions; for the second year, Credit Policy and Practice, Financial Management II, Current Marketing Trends, Economics of Money and Credit; for the third year, Management Policy Seminar, Financial Management Seminar, Development of Executive Leadership, and Timing of Executive Action. A requirement for each student is the Management Study Report—analyzing and if possible solving a problem of benefit to the man and his company. Members of the courses must live in the dormitories on either campus. Fee for each session is $425, which covers tuition, books, room and meals.

Indiana University

The Executive Development Program is concentrated in two summer sessions of three weeks each. It also provides for individual study and development in the period between the sessions. The program for the first year reviews Principles of Business Management, Management of Business Finance, Management of Marketing programs, and Speech Training for Executives. The second year's subjects include Administrative Policy, Personnel and Human Relations, Public and Community Relations, Business-Government Relationships, Personal Financial Problems of the Executive, and Executive Reading. Unique in the Indiana program is the attention given to development of the executive as a person. Thus the subjects also include study of literature, music appreciation and other *humanities*. Evening sessions are also provided on such subjects as "health for the executive." Participants live on the campus, take their meals together. There are no prerequisites in terms of formal education—each applicant is evaluated in terms of previous experience and training, the present position he holds, and his capacity for advancement. Applications come from companies employing the executives, not from the man himself. The company is expected to pay his expenses. Tuition is $500 for each year (includes meals, housing and books).

University of Kansas

The School of Business runs an Executive Development Program for executives for four weeks during the summer months. Classes are scheduled 6 days a week. It is designed to give the executive an opportunity to improve his thought processes and analytical skills. There are no formal educational requirements. Students are nominated by their companies and selected for the classes by the university admissions committee on the basis of securing wide diversification of type of business, industry, geographical area, size of firm and individual experience of the group. Only one person is admitted from each company. All students are expected to live on campus. Subjects covered include Administration of Production and Industrial Relations, Administration of Marketing, Financial Administration, Cost and Accounting Control, Human Relations in Business Administration, Economic, Political and Social Trends, and Industrial Communications. The case method is used and students are also given background reading assignments, as well as an opportunity to improve skills in public speaking, conference leadership, and preparation of business reports.

The course fee is $960, which covers texts, meals and lodging.

Massachusetts Institute of Technology

The Executive Development Program is designed for a small number of exceptionally able young men who are nominated by their employers because they show marked promise of growth into major executive responsibilities. Participation in the program is available only on award of a Sloan Fellowship. The men, who are about one-fourth of the way along in their industrial careers, spend twelve months at M.I.T., studying in depth the fundamentals that underlie sound management action. They are chosen on a competitive basis. The men selected are between 30–35 years of age, with a college degree, and five to ten years of business experience. They must have the enthusiastic support of several levels of their company's management, assurance of a year's leave of absence and of suitable financial aid.

Each man selected for the program is designated a Sloan Fellow and receives a cash award of $1,000 ($2,000 for those living west of the Mississippi River) from the Sloan fund. In addition, about $750 of his expenses are paid for him from the fund. This covers basic costs of seminar dinner meetings and the three extensive group field trips. His company is expected to continue his salary and meet his extra living costs.

Since wives of American executives are considered by M.I.T. to play a large role in building their husbands' success, the men are expected to move their families to Boston for the year.

The twelve-month calendar begins in June, is divided into three periods—summer, fall and spring. The summer program provides a preliminary study of management and economic problems. The work during the balance of the year permits greater depth of analysis. It covers such fields as Accounting Controls, Marketing and Production, Economics and Finance, Industrial Relations and Public Policy, Administrative Policy, Social Science, Human Relations, and Philosophical Aspects of Management Theory.

There are also technical and industrial management seminars.

M.I.T. presents a series of summer courses, running two or three weeks, each directed to a single specific aspect of the general management problem. There are also one-, two- or three-day conferences for management-level personnel.

University of Michigan

Its School of Business Administration offers a four-week Executive Development Program each summer. It is designed for men of recognized capacity, holding positions at or just below the general-management level. Prior academic training is not required. The man must be recommended by his company and accepted by the college. They are selected to form a cross-section of industries, types of experience and executive positions. Classes are held six days a week; combination of textbook and case method is used.

The course fee is $700, covers tuition, books, room and board. It is expected to be paid by the company. Men live in a dormitory on the campus for the period of the session.

Course subjects include Accounting, Business Conditions, Financial Administration, Economics, Human Relations in Management, and Marketing Management.

University of Missouri

The Executive Development Program is a three-year program of advanced study for management personnel. Classes meet once a week. Admission is limited to persons with at least two years of college work and substantial business experience in positions of responsibility. There are twelve courses—two are offered each semester, both meeting the same day. The courses are: Managerial Accounting, Organization and Management, The Individual in the Enterprise, Economics and the Enterprise, Industrial Relations, Money and Banking, Market Management, Managerial Statistics, Financial Management, Government Regulation, and Business Policy. The fee is $35 per course.

University of North Carolina

The School of Business Administration offers a six-month program for advanced study for men in management positions of major responsibility. It consists of eight alternate week ends plus two weeks of full-time residence. Members live and eat together at the Carolina Inn. The group is limited to 23 men. The course covers a series of cases and problems which present situations involving several of the divisions, departments and functions of a business, including business economics; managerial accounting; government and business; banking and money; financial control; labor relations; personnel administration; dynamics of administration. There is no prerequisite of formal college training. Membership fee is $1,000 (includes tuition, meals and lodging). It is expected that the employer will pay the fee.

Northwestern University

The Institute for Management has a four-week, full-time program which runs in three sessions during the summer. Men between 35 and 45 are eligible, without any specific educational prerequisite, but they must be on the policy level in their companies. Groups are limited to about 30 with no more than two men from one company. The program attempts to teach top management point-of-view and method of approach to political, social and economic problems on an overall policy level. Instruction methods include case history, discussions, group conferences, lectures and question periods. It is hoped that the men will develop a logical objective approach to analysis and action in the situations which confront them in top management jobs.

Course fee is $1,000 per man for the four-week period; covers tuition, room, books—but not food. It is customary for firms to continue salaries and provide an expense allowance for executives.

University of Pennsylvania

The Wharton School of Finance and Commerce holds executive conferences on administrative problems each summer. The intensive two-week program uses discussion sessions, panel sessions and problem-solving. Members live and eat on campus for the duration of the course. The conference is designed for executive male personnel who have demonstrated potential for unlimited advancement. Members must be nominated by top management of their companies. Program is devoted to examining the role of the executive with respect to the internal needs of business enterprise, common to all managerial positions, major external forces and factors having sharp impact on management, basic functional areas, an awareness of what is necessary to avoid the narrowing effect of executive specialization. Fee of $600 covers all sessions of the conference, as well as living expenses of the conferees.

University of Pittsburgh

Its Management Problems for Executives is a concentrated eight-week course for men on their way up. It follows the Harvard pattern in that there are no educational prerequisites and the main teaching method is the case study. Subjects covered include Business Policy, Operating and Administrative Policies (finance, business and government, industrial relations, marketing policies, administrative practices), and Management Controls (accounting and industrial management).

The course is aimed at men in their forties who are regarded as having unlimited advancement potential. The sessions are run in the spring and the fall; each is limited to 72 men. The group meets five days a week. Members are required to live at a hotel adjacent to the campus for the duration of the course. For the first two weeks, lectures, discussions and assigned reading matter are used to introduce the subject matter; thereafter the case method and conference meeting discussions are used.

The course fee is $625 (covers tuition and field trips).

Syracuse University

The College of Business Administration offers in two sessions a four-week Executive Controls Program each summer. It is designed "to examine the modern controls function in its broadest aspects to those members of middle management who previously have had little occasion to consider the use of accounting, statistical, financial and budgetary controls in integrating the activities of a business enterprise." The curriculum is presented as an integrated unit rather than as a series of separate subjects, and includes: Accounting (analysis of accounting and financial data, budgeting, cost accounting, internal auditing), Financial Management (use of accounting data by management, cash budgeting, replacement of equipment, sources of financing), Human Relations (control within an organization, motivating behavior), Statistical Controls (every-day tools for measurement, forecasting, sampling and quality con-trols), Sales Control (sales forecast, product planning, control of distribution costs), Production Planning and Control (integration of sales and production objectives, production planning, control of production), and Business Policy. The course is designed to teach management to know better when and how to utilize the particular skills of the "figure men," rather than to develop competence in their use.

The course is aimed at men from 30 to 45 years of age, who are selected from a variety of businesses to provide the diversity of management experience essential to provocative discussion. No more than two men from a company are permitted in any one ses-sion. Maximum of 26 men per session. Lectures, case studies and panel presentations are used in instruction. Classes run six days a week, morning and afternoon. Course fee is $1,000 for the four weeks, includes tuition, books, room and board.

University of Texas

The Executive Development Program lasts for five weeks, is conducted at the Bar K Ranch on Lake Travis, 32 miles from Austin. It is designed for executives immediately below the top-management level, covers subjects like attitudes and human be-havior; business and society; labor relations; managerial account-ing; marketing management; organization and management. The case method predominates, but the course also uses panels, role-playing, informal discussion. visual aids, lecture-forums, personal consultation. Classes are scheduled five days a week, with after-din-ner discussions and conferences. Classroom assignments are given which require about four hours of preparation each day. There are no formal education prerequisites. Companies nominate men to the program, pay their expenses and continue their salaries. Fee is $900 (includes tuition, texts, room and meals). Program is limited to 24 men, who are screened by the Admissions Committee.

There is also a program of Executive Seminars designed for executives immediately below the top-management level in small and medium-sized enterprises. Each seminar runs a week; four seminars are scheduled each year. Participants stay together with no allowance for time off during the conference. The fee is $175 for each seminar (includes tuition, room and meals). Conferences are limited to 24 men sponsored by their companies. The seminars are scheduled for one week in February, April, July and November each year.

University of Washington

The Advanced Management Seminar is held each summer for six weeks. There are no educational requirements. The group is limited to 30 members, no more than two from any one company. Members must live on campus and be free of business and social obligations. Areas studied are Administrative Controls, Financial Management, Policy Determination, The Human Element in Administration, and Oral and Written Communication. Case and committee methods are used. Participants are commonly 35–40 years of age, earning about $10,000. Cost of seminar is $1,000 (covers tuition, room and board), plus $200 registration fee. Companies sponsoring men for the seminar pay the costs and continue the men's salaries.

Banff School of Advanced Management (Banff, Alberta, Canada)

The Course in Advanced Management is designed for executives who are nominated and sent by their companies; ages range between 25 and 50 with the optimum between 28 and 45. Enrollment is limited to 70 students. Subject matter is concerned with executive action—functions, responsibilities and actions which executives must take in the course of their daily work. The course uses a combination of case, seminar and lecture methods on the theory that people learn by doing. Talks by prominent Canadian businessmen, texts, and films supplement the training. Subjects covered include General Administration (administrative action, discipline as an aspect of organization, business research and communication), Business Functions (marketing, production management, financing enterprise, financial and accounting controls), and Industrial Relations (human relations in industry, labor relations, public relations).

Course fee is $690 including tuition, room and board, texts. Men live, study and eat together. The course is under the joint sponsorship of the Universities of Alberta, British Columbia, Manitoba and Saskatchewan. Quotas are allocated to each of the four Western Provinces, Eastern Canada and the United States.

University of Toronto (Toronto, Ontario, Canada)

The Institute of Business Administration offers an Administrative Development Program through a series of evening sessions throughout the winter on subjects in the field of administration. Most of the subjects are covered on a seminar basis, with special lecturers drawn from the business community. There are no educational prerequisites. Sessions are held one evening a week, twenty sessions for each subject. Students may take as many subjects as they can attend. Fee is $40 per subject. Subjects include Administrative Practices, Administrative and Financial Controls, Marketing, Production Management, Managerial Economics, Case Studies of Human Problems in Administration, Administration of Collective Agreements, Personnel Psychology, and Marketing Research. The college feels that the program gives men who are expected to assume higher responsibilities an opportunity to prepare themselves through advanced study in administration by a planned program extending over several years.

Seminars and Conferences

In addition to the formal executive development programs, there are many courses available in the various colleges and universities which are aimed at increasing executive know-how. These cover the methods of planning, organization and control involved in management. Many of them are held in the evening, do not require any specific educational background. To find out what is available in your locality, consult the catalogue of the college which is convenient, and look through the offerings in the School or Division of General Studies, General Education or Business Administration.

In addition to the courses provided by the colleges and universities, the trade associations frequently schedule seminars or conferences covering management topics. Some of the best known of these are the American Management Association and the National Industrial Conference Board. These seminars are held in cities throughout the country and usually involve from two days to a week of concentrated lecture-and-discussion of the subject scheduled for consideration. Attendance at these courses is useful mainly for lower or middle-management personnel, to increase their grasp of the various factors involved in management decisions. The men also have opportunities to make contacts and exchange experiences with executives from other companies and in other businesses, which are very helpful in broadening their scope.

Universities are paying increased attention to programs for development of executives, and many are planning new programs to meet the needs of companies in their areas. If you are interested in using college classes as a supplement to your company's efforts to develop its people, contact your local college. Frequently the programs discussed above were developed to meet the interest shown by local industries. Many of the courses were originally co-sponsored by a group of local companies—some are still on that basis. They work closely with the companies in developing the course materials, schedules, speakers, etc. If your local college does not have executive development programs or courses suitable for your business needs, your interest may be instrumental in securing addition of courses to the school's curriculum.